THE
FLYING
BOOK

DAVID BLATNER

GREYSTONE BOOKS

Douglas & McIntyre Publishing Group
Vancouver/Toronto

THE FLYING BOOK

EVERYTHING YOU'VE EVER WONDERED ABOUT FLYING ON AIRPLANES

FOR MY MOTHER, BARBARA BLATNER-FIKES,

WHO TAUGHT ME TO ALWAYS ASK QUESTIONS.

Greystone Books
A division of Douglas & McIntyre Ltd.
2323 Quebec Street, Suite 201
Vancouver, B.C. V5T 4S7
www.greystonebooks.com

Originated by Walker Publishing Company, Inc., U.S.A.

National Library of Canada Cataloguing in Publication Data
Blatner, David
  The flying book/David Blatner.

  ISBN 1-55054-992-8

  1. Air travel. 2. Aeronautics. I. Title.
HE9776.B52 2003   387.7   C2002-911304-0

The line art on p.iv is an illustration of Jacob Degen's
Flugmaschine, Vienna 1807.

Book design by
Maura Fadden Rosenthal/Mspace
Printed in Canada by Friesens
Printed on acid-free paper

The highest anyone has ever jumped into the air is 8 feet .5 inches (2.4 meters).

Oh, I have slipped the surly bonds of the earth

And danced the skies of laughter-silver wings;

Sunward I've climbed, and joined the tumbling mirth

Of sun-split clouds—and done a hundred things

You have not dreamed of—wheeled and soared and swung

Hung in the sunlit silence. Hov'ring there,

I've chased the shouting wind along, and flung

My eager craft through footless halls of air.

Up, up the long, delirious burning blue

I've topped the windswept heights with easy grace

Where never lark, or even eagle flew.

And, while with silent, lifting mind I've trod

The high untrespassed sanctity of space,

Put out my hand, and touched the face of God.

—Pilot Officer John Gillespie Magee, Jr. Royal Canadian Air Force

CONTENTS

The airplane has unveiled for us the true face of
the earth.

—Antoine de Saint-Exupéry,
WIND, SAND, AND STARS

He rode upon a cherub, and did fly: yea, he did
fly upon the wings of the wind.

—Psalms 18:10

ACKNOWLEDGMENTS

It is a pleasure to acknowledge the kind and generous help I have received from so many people in the process of writing this book. Special thanks go to my editor, Liza Blue, my agent, Reid Boates, book designer Maura Rosenthal, and the folks at Walker & Company, including George Gibson and Marlene Tungseth. My lead technical reviewers, Captain Cal MacDonald and Captain Sandy Niles, provided help beyond the call of duty. For behind-the-scenes glimpses of airline operations, I'd especially like to thank Jack Walsh, Barbara Balatico, and pilots Chris Mennella and Craig Wirfs at Alaska Airlines; John Hotard and Ben Kristy at American Airlines; and Michael Olsen and Don Martin at Delta Airlines.

For answers to an unending stream of questions, thanks to Don Sellers, Scott Eberhardt, Jef Raskin, Paul Stern, Keith Hagstette, J. C. Cuevas, Brian Lawler, Jim Sugar, Jack Tinkel; Kristine Kaske and Bob Dreesen at the archives of the Smithsonian Air and Space Museum, Jack Walker at the NASM restoration facility; Janice Baker at the Seattle Museum of Flight; and Sandra Angers and Debbie Heathers at Boeing Corporation. My great appreciation also to the folks at the Seattle-Tacoma Fear of Flying Clinic, Barbara Schaetti, and the baristas at Diva Espresso and various Starbucks locations who helped provide the steam to keep going.

Finally, my deepest thanks to my wife, Debbie, our son, Gabriel, and my parents, Barbara Blatner-Fikes, Richard Fikes, Adam and Allee Blatner, and Don and Snookie Carlson, for their never-ending support and love.

Besnier's attempt to fly, 1678.

INTRODUCTION
THE JOY OF FLYING

One of the most fascinating facts about flying in airplanes is that while almost everybody does it, relatively few people really understand how it works. True, most people who drive aren't automotive engineers either, but it's not difficult to intuit more or less how a car works. Airplanes, on the other hand, just seem like magic.

Although flying isn't actually magic, it *is* like a really good magic trick. Like plucking a rabbit from a hat, pilots use precision and excellent timing to succeed in pulling off a stunt that is plainly, obviously impossible and yet somehow works. Our bodies do their part to sustain a sense of illusion: Our organs weren't designed to handle the conflicting sensations we feel in flight, so it can feel like you're dropping when the aircraft is actually rising, and you can fly in circles and not feel the turn. Airlines do their part, too, by creating a carefully controlled environment: You take a seat in a room with small windows, have dinner, maybe watch a movie, and when you leave you just happen to find yourself in a new city.

Some folks love suspending their disbelief and sit happily trusting that their 800,000-pound jumbo jet will lift off the ground and safely take them to their destination. Most people, however, sit with a certain amount of tension, uncomfortable with trusting their lives to what looks like a trick. Flying is one area in which ignorance is often *not* bliss, but rather causes a general sense of anxiety among many travelers. In fact, studies show that as few as one in seventeen are totally comfortable when flying, and as many as one in every six people (about 5 million people in Canada) avoid flying whenever possible.

Are those wings supposed to be flexing up and down like that? What was that thump? Will this air turbulence make us crash? What are those pilots doing up there, anyway? These are common questions, even for people who fly frequently. Fortunately, unlike a magic trick, the more you know about how flying works, the more you can actually enjoy it. That's where this book comes in.

The Unbelievable Dream

One hundred years ago almost nobody on Earth believed that humans would ever be able to fly in heavier-than-air machines. Many prominent scientists proclaimed it impossible and urged aviation researchers to focus instead on more efficient hydrogen-filled balloons to carry passengers from city to city. Their skepticism isn't surprising; after all, to fly is perhaps humankind's oldest dream, and several thousand years of failed attempts are likely to cause more than a bit of doubt.

Historically, the great disappointment that humans couldn't fly (seemingly the only thing that we couldn't achieve) translated into the widespread belief that the sky was reserved for the gods. Excavations from ancient Egypt reveal gods and goddesses with wings. There are old Taoist stories of holy men being lifted to the next world by cranes. The Greek philosopher Plato wrote, "The natural function of the wing is to soar upwards and carry that which is heavy up to the place where dwells the race of gods." And who can forget the Greek tragedy of Icarus, who fell to Earth after his wings melted in the heat of the sun?

Later, Christian tradition held that angels had wings, and that God stopped Satan from flying by clipping his. Muslims believe that Muhammad was raised to Heaven for a night by a winged horse. In the second millennia, the ability to fly

became associated with witchcraft, and images of witches on broomsticks filled many people's hearts with fear. (Today, the great success of the *Harry Potter* stories places both witches and flying broomsticks in a much kinder light.)

> *In our dreams we are able to fly . . . and that is a remembering of how we were meant to be.*
> —*Madeleine L'Engle*,
> WALKING ON WATER

Even the Wright brothers' historic first powered flight in 1903 couldn't undo the emotional impact of 3,000 years of human myths. In fact, the invention of the airplane only added to the soup by offering a double-edged sword: On the one side, flying gives people control over their lives, letting them move around the planet faster than ever before; on the other side, it removes passengers from control, opening a Pandora's box of concerns.

Twentieth-century Hollywood captured these mixed emotions beautifully, generating a whole new panoply of flying myths. For instance, in the 1950s, the modern-day television hero Sky King could swoop from the sky to overcome villains on the ground. Around the same time, the *Twilight Zone* showed a young William Shatner battling an elusive gremlin on the wing outside his window, who threatened to crash the airplane. (John Lithgow played this role in the movie of the same name.) The "gremlin" still perfectly reflects many passenger's irrational fears that develop from misunderstandings about turbulence and why airplanes fly. Over forty years later, many people still find themselves haunted by these televised images.

The Revealed Mystery

Of course, flying offers more than a method of travel and a bucket of worries; flying has offered a whole new perspective on our planet and an entirely new way of living our lives. Early pilots noticed that while in flight they could see patterns on the ground that were previously hidden—patterns that revealed secrets. During the First World War, pilots found evidence of old Mesopotamian ruins from the air, and the field of aerial archaeology was born. Similarly, it was only through the use of airplanes that modern geologists and geographers have been able to map and explain many aspects of our planet.

Today, any passenger can look out an airplane window and discover patterns that no preflight human ever saw. Twisting, searching rivers and ravines snake like immense fractal branches across the countryside. . . . The high desert displays its glory in 100-mile-long stripes of orange iridescence. . . . The sharp teeth of mountaintops poke through the shimmering early morning clouds.

Flying also provides a new perspective on our own civilization. Grand skyscrapers are surprisingly small when seen from an airplane, and their rooftops are often sadly mundane. Conversely, farmlands that seem boring from the ground can take on amazing checkerboard patterns from the sky. As an airplane ascends, everyday objects like cars and houses begin to appear like toys. Then later, at higher altitudes, they become so small that whole cities appear like pieces of a patchwork quilt scattered across the land. Photographs of the Earth from space reveal the ultimate pattern that powered flight offers us: We are all one.

The Flying Book

Flying is possible. It's not magic. It's not even a magic trick. The rules of flight are relatively simple, though they can appear overwhelming at first. This book is dedicated to explaining everything you might want to know about flying on commercial airlines—from how airplanes get off the ground, to where your luggage goes after you hand it over at the ticket counter, from how airplanes are built and maintained, to what the pilots are doing behind the cockpit door.

Note the word *commercial*. That means this book doesn't cover the details of military or general (private, small airplane) aviation. This leaves out a lot: By some reports, of the more than 220,000 airplanes registered in the United States and Canada, about 95 percent of them fall into the general aviation category. Nevertheless, the vast majority of flyers are passengers, not pilots. So while this book will be of interest to many pilots, it's the passengers who will benefit the most. Note also that amounts of money are given in U.S. dollars and that "federal" refers to the U.S. government.

You can read the book from front to back, or skip around to the chapters that interest you most. The important thing is that you enjoy both the book and your flight. So sit back, relax, and take it all in.

VOL/FLIGHT :
RK 30

PORTE/GATE :

NOMBRE BAG CABINE

SIEGE/SEAT :
3F

NOM/NAME :

SIEGE/SEAT :
3F

PART. :

DE/FROM :

CARTE D'ACCES A BORD/BOARDING PASS

F

AIR AFRIQUE

British
airways
Concord

Boarding pass
Carte d'accès à bord
Einsteigekarte.
Tarjeta de embarque

seat
7S

date
19/5

flight
BA173

seat

no smok

service information

name

Flight

SK503

BOARDI
FIRST C
Please present at
15 minutes before

seat
7B

Name

SAS
SCANDINAVIAN AIRLINES

1241

It is not necessarily impossible for human beings
to fly, but it so happens that God did not give
them the knowledge of how to do it. It follows,
therefore, that anyone who claims that he can
fly must have sought the aid of the devil. To
attempt to fly is therefore sinful.

—Roger Bacon,
thirteenth-century Franciscan friar

HOW DO AIRPLANES WORK?

There are a number of things that people do everyday that appear to be plainly impossible upon closer examination. For instance, any non-deaf person can hear sound. However, the *reason* you can hear sound is almost beyond belief. Sound travels because air molecules (which are themselves about 1/100,000 the size of the tiniest speck of dust you can see) bounce into each other like waves rippling on a pond until they reach your ear, where they encounter tiny hairs deep inside your ear that bend with infinitesimally small movements. You hear noises depending on *which* hairs bend and by how much.

Similarly, it's obvious that airplanes can fly. But how? In the next few chapters, you'll see that aircraft (and birds) fly on those same, invisible air molecules, and that airplane wings, engines, and so on, are all designed to take advantage of these mysterious but powerful forces of nature. Don't worry; learning how flying works may take away the mystery, but it takes nothing away from the wonder.

HOW AIRPLANES FLY

If you could read minds, the question you'd hear most often at an airport would be, "How is this thing going to get off the ground?" Whether you're sitting on the aircraft or watching it from the ground, the idea that a hulking Boeing 747 weighing almost a million pounds could lift off the ground and fly several thousand miles seems not only improbable but simply impossible. Yet obviously, airplanes do fly. And if there's anything more astonishing than the fact that these behemoths can fly, it is *how* they do it. In fact, the more you learn about how airplanes fly, the less possible it seems.

Of course, any physical action, when investigated too closely, leads to doubt. Have you ever stopped to consider how you walk? Your left leg moves forward until you're about to fall, but your foot nimbly catches you while your right leg swings forward, shifting your weight into equilibrium. . . . The more you think about the hundreds of tiny physical adjustments that must be made each second—the impulses moving through nerves, the pumping of oxygenated blood to the legs, the flexing of the abdominal muscles, and so on—the more shocking it is that we can pull it off.

Sir James Matthew Barrie, best known for his play *Peter Pan*, once wrote that the "reason birds can fly and we can't is simply that they have perfect faith, for to have faith is to have wings." Fortunately, faith alone doesn't keep airplanes in the sky. The explanation is much more mystifying.

Don't Rely on Bernoulli

Almost everyone learns in elementary or secondary school that airplanes fly because of something called the *Bernoulli effect:* The wings are curved on top and flat on the bottom, forcing the air to travel farther, and therefore faster, over the wing than under it. Eighteenth-century Swiss mathematician Daniel Bernoulli discovered that the faster a fluid moves, the lower its pressure. The result: There's less pressure above the wing than under it, and so the airplane gets sucked upward into the sky.

Unfortunately, this is only part of the explanation; it doesn't describe how airplanes can fly upside down, or how airplanes with wings that have little or no camber (difference in curve between the top and bottom) can fly at all. This oversimplified interpretation of the Bernoulli effect also implies that the air moving over and under the wing must magically "rejoin" at the trailing edge of the wing (some teachers say the air moves over the wing faster so that it can "catch up" with the air moving under the wing). Wind tunnel experiments show that this is a fallacy—surprisingly, the air above the wings accellerates so quickly that it actually reaches the back of the wing *before* the air below the wings.

Don't feel bad if you have relied on this "simplified Bernoulli" explanation up to now—even the famous physicist Albert Einstein was fooled into believing it. In 1917, when Einstein was hired by a prominent German airplane company to design a new, highly aerodynamic wing, he created the *cat's back airfoil*—a nearly triangular wing that forced air to travel much farther over the top of the wing than under it. After it was tested and shown to be spectacularly ineffective, Einstein was never again asked to design aircraft parts. Years later, he admitted that his was a failure of "a man who thinks a lot but reads little."

What Einstein (and so many teachers and textbooks before and after him) ignored is that the real reason that airplanes go up ("generate lift") is simply that they push air down.

What Goes Up Always Pushes Down

The most important thing to keep in mind if you want to understand how airplanes fly is that the air around us acts just like a liquid. We breath this "liquid," we walk through this "liquid," and in a balloon we can float in this "liquid." The only way to raise yourself when you're treading water is by pushing water down. An airplane rises in much the same way: by pushing the air around it down.

There are airplanes that can take off vertically by directing the exhaust from their jet engines down toward the ground (called VTOLs, for Vertical Take Off and Landing aircraft). They are literally pushing air down, which results in the airplane going up. Most airplanes, however, use a different technique to move air down.

Airplane wings push air down in the same way that a rudder on a boat works: by deflecting the fluid that's rushing by. Of course, a boat's rudder moves water to the left or right whereas a wing moves air up or down, but the principle is the same. The trick is to point the trailing edge of the wing in the direction you want the air to go (usually down). As air flows over and under the wing, it gets deflected downward.

Air follows the shape of the wing (top). Increasing the angle of attack entrains the air farther down (bottom).

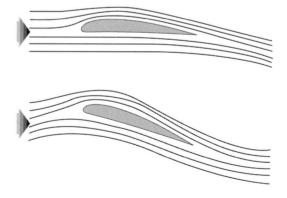

The Bernoulli effect says that when water is forced through a narrow area, the water's speed increases and the pressure drops. Similarly, air speeds up when it travels over a wing, and as it speeds up the air molecules are spread more thinly over the wing. The thinner the air, the fewer molecules press against any one point on the wing. The fewer molecules pressing, the lower the pressure.

Sir Isaac Newton's third law of physics states that for every action there is an equal and opposite action. So as the air moves down, the wings rise up and take the rest of the airplane with them.

How to Train the Air

If you stick your hand out of a car window while driving down the road, fingers raised at a slight angle against the oncoming wind, your hand will be pushed up because it is deflecting air down. In this case, the majority of the lift (the power that's raising your hand) comes from the air deflected off your palm. It turns out that this is a relatively inefficient way to create lift—think about how fast the car needs to be moving before you feel the effect.

Strangely enough, most lift acting on an airplane wing doesn't come from air deflected off the bottom but from air flowing over the wing's *top* surface. In other words, airplanes don't fly like kites or parasails; airplanes gain lift in a completely different way.

Remember that air is like a liquid, and liquid is slightly "sticky." When you pour a fluid (like tea) out of a carafe too slowly, it sticks to the carafe and dribbles out onto the table, right? This tendency for liquid to follow the shape of an object is called the *Coanda effect*, and it explains why air moving over the top of the wing gets "pulled down" along the shape of the wing. Because the trailing edge of the wing is pointed slightly downward, the air passing over the wing flows in that same downward direction. The Coanda effect essentially helps the wing push air down.

This is nonintuitive, so try the following experiment: Use two fingers to hold a teaspoon by the end of its handle upside down over a sink. Now turn the faucet all the way on and gently bring the underside of the spoon against the rushing water. As

Those dimples on a golf ball actually trap the air and help it to better follow the surface of the ball. When a ball has backspin, the air traveling over the ball is entrained toward the ground, which helps the ball stay in flight longer, similar to an airplane wing (though wings are so big, they don't need dimples).

soon as the spoon touches the water, the liquid sticks to the curved surface and shoots diagonally down off the spoon. The result: The spoon gets "pushed" in the opposite direction, into the water stream. If you turn your head sideways (and squint your eyes), you can sort of see the spoon as a wing getting pushed up into the air rushing by.

Here's where the Bernoulli principle kicks in. As the air is entrained along the top of the wing, it is "pulled" down and back, causing both a drop in pressure and an increase in speed. The lowest pressure occurs where the air is diverted the most: just behind the wing's curved leading edge. The air is deflected downward, the pressure drops above the wing, and the aircraft rises.

Attacking the Air

Raising your fingers against the oncoming wind as you put your hand out a car window is called raising the *angle of attack* in aviation terms, and the more you raise the angle, the more lift you get (the faster your hand goes up). Similarly, when you raise a wing's angle of attack (pointing the nose of the airplane up, for instance), you get more lift because the air is deflected downward faster. The trick to flying a plane upside down is in keeping the front edge of the wing higher than the back edge in order to deflect air down (toward the ground) and create lift.

However, there's a problem: Air is sticky, but it's not *that* sticky, so beyond a certain angle the Coanda effect stops working and the air won't follow the top surface of the wing anymore. At this point—called *stall*—the air no longer gets deflected downward, and the wing can no longer generate lift. On most airplanes, stall begins when the angle of attack is greater than about fifteen degrees. (Note that the lift doesn't just suddenly disappear; it's a gradual process that can be reversed by dipping the nose of the aircraft down.)

When fighter jets zoom up into the air at steep angles, their lift is based more on their powerful engines (which act almost like rockets) than on their wings. Commercial jet airliners and smaller aircraft, however, have to rise slowly in order to keep from stalling.

A Delicate Balance

Some people don't like thinking about details, like how extraordinary it is that algae in the ocean account for much of the oxygen we breathe, or that thoughts are technically the result of brain cells passing chemicals to each other 1 million times a second. When we look too closely, we find that every moment of our lives is based on a delicate balance among mysterious forces that can be dimly grasped but hardly believed. Airplanes can fly because we humans have learned how to manipulate the air around us and hang in that balance.

When you hear that an airplane flies at 500 mph (800 km/hr), that's the speed at which the air is traveling over the wings (*airspeed*), not necessarily how fast the airplane is moving over the ground (*ground speed*). An airplane flying into a headwind is like a boat traveling upstream—it takes longer to cover the same distance. For example, an airplane flying with an airspeed of 500 mph into a 50-mph headwind would have a ground speed of only 450 mph. But flying with a 50-mph tailwind boosts the ground speed to 550 mph, getting you to your destination faster.

Ignorance is the curse of God.
Knowledge is the wing wherewith we fly
to heaven.
      —William Shakespeare, HENRY IV,
                part 2, act 4, scene 7

WHAT IS AIR?

The only reason it is hard to understand how a fully loaded jet aircraft can fly is that air is invisible. If water were invisible, you might have a harder time believing that an ocean liner could float or a penguin could swim. And yet, air is as real and substantive as water. You can't see the air, but you can see and feel its effects: grass moving in a gentle breeze, objects flying through the air in a hurricane, the steady erosion of rock along a windy beach.

Air is a relatively thick syrup of oxygen and nitrogen, along with some water vapor and a smattering of other elements. Like everything else, air is affected by gravity, so it has weight. However, the weight of air changes depending on a number of factors, including temperature (hot air is lighter than cold air) and humidity (believe it or not, the higher the humidity, the lighter the air, because the molecules in water vapor are actually lighter than the weight of the gases in dry air). The weight also depends on air pressure, which is greater at sea level than it is at the top of a mountain because at higher altitudes there is less atmosphere "pushing down."

Technically, air is very light (one cubic foot of it at sea level weighs about 1.25 ounces, or thirty-five grams), but it actually exerts an incredible amount of pressure because there is so much of it. At sea level,

The airplane stays up because it doesn't have time to fall.

—Orville Wright

Airplanes can fly because they push the air around them down. A Boeing 737 weighing 150,000 pounds (68,000 kg) must deflect about 88,000 pounds (40,000 kg) of air—over a million cubic feet (31,500 cubit meters)—down by 55 feet (16.75 m) each second while in flight.

every object touching the air (including your skin) experiences about 14.7 pounds of pressure per square inch (or about 1 kilogram per square centimeter). That's like tons of weight pressing against your skin each moment! However, you can't feel it because you

have air pressure inside you, too. We're all so used to this equilibrium that it is difficult to feel the air around us.

Seeing Air

Although air is full of molecules, it's invisible not just because the molecules are too small to see, but also because they don't reflect or absorb the light waves that humans can see. On the other hand, you can see water vapor (like clouds), dust, or pollution particles suspended in the air.

For example, airplanes make clouds called *contrails* (condensation trails) at high altitudes when water vapor latches on to tiny particles in the engine exhaust. These long clouds can dissipate quickly or last for hours, depending on the humidity and the wind conditions.

Similarly, plumes of cloud can appear when an airplane flies in relatively humid air—that is, air carrying water vapor. Air traveling over the wings is moving faster and at a lower pressure than the air around it, and lower air pressure forces the water vapor to rapidly condense into clouds. These low-pressure plumes typically appear at takeoff or landing, either over the wings or at the tips of the wings. (You can also see these kinds of clouds as wind blows over tall buildings or mountains.)

You can also sometimes see the air where areas of cool and hot air meet (like the air above an asphalt road in the summer) because light travels slightly faster through the less dense hot air than it does through cool air. The result is a shimmering "mirage." The air may fool the eye, but it's as real as anything. So the next time you find yourself on an airplane wondering what's between you and the ground, try imagining you're a fish surrounded by clear water that you can't see, but which is supporting you nevertheless.

One of the most joyous experiences when flying is breaking through the cloud layer into the blue sky above. The above–the–clouds perspective can be fascinating, especially if you know what to look for. Here's a rundown of the basic types of clouds you might see, either from an airplane window or from the ground

LOW CLOUDS. The lowest clouds in the sky generally consist of water droplets. *Stratus* clouds are the lowest of the clouds and don't have well–defined edges. (You can think of fog as stratus clouds at ground level.) The word *stratus* comes from the Latin "to stretch or extend." *Cumulus* clouds are the opposite: Fluffy and popcornlike, these are the most stereotypical of clouds (the name comes from the Latin "to heap or pile"). Although cumulus clouds appear serene, they typically appear in more turbulent air than the truly calm stratus clouds. Another low-flying cloud is the *cap* cloud (sometimes also called a wave cloud), which appears over mountains or even some tall buildings.

MIDDLE CLOUDS. Clouds at 7,000 to 18,000 feet are thicker, consisting of ice crystals or water droplets. *Altocumulus* clouds look like a thick textured fabric, perhaps canvas, or a wool blanket. *Altostratus* clouds are more diffuse and uniform, like a blotchy cotton sheet.

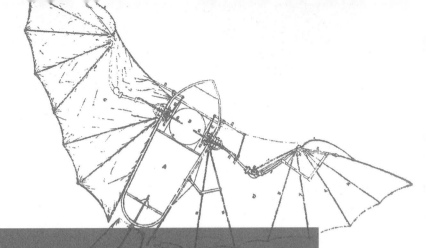

HIGH CLOUDS. The highest clouds in the sky are composed of ice crystals and appear above 18,000 feet, sometimes even at airliner cruise altitudes (around 28,000–35,000 feet). From the ground you can see the sun or moon through these clouds (sometimes with halos around them). *Cirrus* clouds are thin, wispy, and often gently curved liked hairs in the sky; in fact *cirrus* is Latin for a "curl" or "fringe." *Cirrocumulus* clouds are like a thin sheet of delicate textured fabric, like wavy cotton gauze. *Cirrostratus* clouds are more diffuse and blurrier, blanketing the sky like wax paper.

MULTILAYER CLOUDS. Thick and dark storm clouds are typically made of *nimbostratus* clouds, which may reach from the low to the middle strata. *Cumulonimbus* clouds, perhaps the most dramatic–looking of clouds, tower into the sky, sometimes as high as 60,000 feet, often with a characteristic anvil–shaped head. These clouds can produce lightning, thunder, hail, heavy rain, and extremely strong winds, and pilots go out of their way to fly around them.

Aviation is proof, that given the will, we have the capacity to achieve the impossible.
—*Captain Edward "Eddie" Rickenbacker*

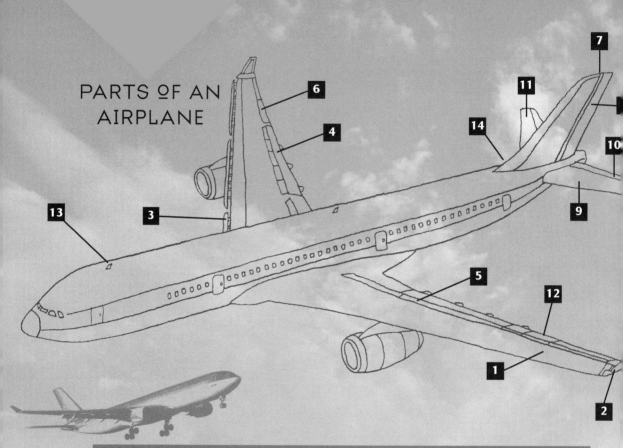

PARTS OF AN AIRPLANE

Why can't an airliner's doors open during flight? Because they're actually wider than the door frame itself. At the gate, the door first opens inward, then rotates, then slips sideways out of the frame. However, there's no way to open a door when an airliner is flying at cruise altitude because the air inside a jet airliner is pressurized to about seven pounds per square inch and the ambient outside air at 35,000 feet is about 3.5 pounds per square inch. Even the smallest exit door covers about 650 square inches; opening one of these would be like lifting a 2,200-pound weight. Airline doors—also called *plug doors*—are designed so they can be opened even with a quarter-inch (7 mm) of ice covering the outside of the airplane.

1. **Wings:** The wings are cambered (somewhat curved on top and flat on the bottom) and are slightly higher at the tips (*dihedral*), giving the airplane additional stability and strength.

2. **Winglets:** An upturned wing tip is called a winglet. In some aircraft, winglets can increase efficiency (you can fly farther on less fuel) by reducing the amount of air that spirals up from underneath the wing. *Blended winglets* are extensions that curve smoothly up at a smaller angle than normal winglets.

3. **Slats:** At takeoff and landing, the pilots extend the slats at the front edge of the wing, effectively extending the wing so that it can fly better at slower speeds. These are usually found on larger jets.

4. **Flaps:** The pilots extend the flaps along the trailing edge of the wings at takeoff and landing for the same reasons birds spread their feathers: for increased lift at slow speeds. During flight, the pilots retract the flaps and slats for a more streamlined wing.

5. **Spoilers:** Flat panels along the top edges of the wings that, when raised, "spoil" some of the lift by creating drag. The pilots can raise the spoilers on both wings in flight to descend faster, or raise one wing's spoilers to help turn the aircraft. Both spoilers pop up at full force as soon as the airplane lands to keep the airplane firmly on the runway. Some people also call spoilers *speed brakes*.

6. **Ailerons:** The pilots roll the airplane to the left or right by raising one aileron and lowering the other, which deflects the air up or down. (The ailerons typically move only a few inches, even on a jumbo jet.) The pilots turn the aircraft by adjusting both the ailerons and the rudder.

7. **Vertical stabilizer:** The part of the tail that sticks straight up and helps the airplane fly straight, like the tail feathers on an arrow. Some high-tech aircraft, like the stealth bomber, don't have a tail. On a paper airplane, the vertical stabilizer usually descends from the bottom.

8. **Rudder:** The rudder on an airplane works just like a rudder on a boat: by deflecting the air to the left or the right. Turning the rudder to the left turns the tail to the right and the front of the airplane to the left, causing the aircraft to slip slightly sideways through the sky. The pilots normally turn the airplane through the sky by adjusting both the rudder and the ailerons.

9. **Horizontal stabilizers:** A set of smaller wings on the tail that offset the lift of the primary wings just enough to balance the airplane so it doesn't pitch up or down. The pilots usually adjust the angle of the horizontal stabilizer before takeoff based on the weight and balance of the airplane.

10. **Elevators:** Control surfaces that attach to the trailing edge of the horizontal stabilizers and, when adjusted, change the pitch or attitude of the airplane (causing the nose of the aircraft to move up or down). Just before takeoff, the elevators are pivoted up slightly, pushing the tail down and the nose up.

11. **Trim tabs:** Small surfaces at the trailing edges of the ailerons, horizontal stabilizer, and rudder that help balance the airplane. For instance, if the balance is slightly too far back and the nose of the airplane is tending to raise up, the pilots can adjust the trim tabs to counteract this tendency, bringing the airplane back into level flight.

12. **Static wicks:** The friction of air moving over the skin of the aircraft builds up a static electrical charge. Small extensions called static wicks look like antennas along the trailing edge of the wings and tail release that charge into the air.

13. **Antennae:** Three or four small fins spaced out along the top and bottom of the fuselage. Antennas are used for air traffic control communication, inter-company communication, navigation, and so on.

14. **Empennage:** The entire tail section of the airplane (pronounced "em-pa-**najh**").

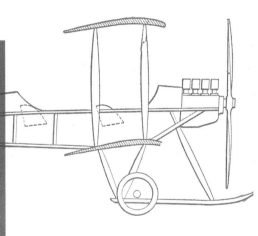

Did you know that the propellers on most propeller–driven airplanes can be rotated while in motion? At takeoff, when the need for thrust is greatest, the propellers are set at a low angle so they're almost perpendicular with the oncoming air. At cruise altitude, the pilots adjust the propellers so that they're at a fairly sharp angle (closer to parallel with the airflow). It was the Wright brothers who first realized that propellers should be shaped like small wings (*airfoils*) that are twisted so they have a large angle of attack near the center and a small angle of attack at their edges. This way, they actually both push air back and pull the airplane forward.

The Concorde and other aircraft with *delta wings* (wings that look like giant triangles, or the Greek letter Delta) don't have slats and flaps because their wide wings are already good at flying at low speeds. However, these wings also cause a lot of drag, forcing the Concorde to fly at much higher altitudes, where the air is thinner.

When describing airplanes in flight, it's helpful to remember three terms:

▼ PITCH: The movement of the nose of the aircraft up or down; also called the airplane's *attitude*.

▼ ROLL: The movement of each wing up or down.

▼ YAW: The movement of the tail pivoting to the left or right.

Airplanes can adjust each of these angles separately or simultaneously. When turning, airplanes typically roll and yaw; plus, to maintain altitude, the pitch is increased slightly.

Look closely at the exterior of an airplane, near the nose, and you'll find several oddly shaped sensors like angle of attack vanes and air temperature probes. *Static ports* are circular and set flush with the fuselage so that air flows across them. *Pitot tubes* are L-shaped so that they capture air flowing directly into them. The faster the airplane travels, the more pressure builds up in the Pitot tube. However, the static port always registers the ambient air pressure. By measuring the difference in air pressure between the Pitot tubes and static ports, the airplane's computer can determine true airspeed.

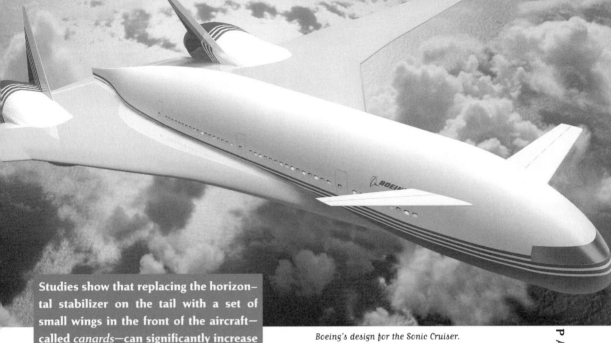

Boeing's design for the Sonic Cruiser.

Studies show that replacing the horizontal stabilizer on the tail with a set of small wings in the front of the aircraft—called *canards*—can significantly increase efficiency. A few business jets have canards, and Boeing's design for the now-scrapped, futuristic Sonic Cruiser aircraft incorporates them.

The large bulbous objects hanging under the wings (no, not the jet engines; the other things) are called *canoe farings* because of their boatlike shape. They enclose the bulky mechanisms that extend and retract the flaps and slats during flight.

Airplanes must have a red light at their left (port) wing tip and a green light at their right (starboard) wing tip. This rule extends back as far as 1864 when the British navy first started placing red and green lights on their ships. Airplanes also typically have a brightly flashing white light that makes them easier to distinguish at night. Sometimes, when flying in or near storm clouds, passengers mistake this flash of light for lightning.

If you look closely at the top of a jet airliner's wings, you'll probably find a row of small metal tabs standing about one inch (2.5 cm) tall, especially in front of the ailerons. These are *vortex generators*, which actually help the air follow the shape of the wing during flight by creating tiny whirl-winds over the wing. You can sometimes find vortex generators on the tail in front of the rudder, too.

Airline windows are built with two or three layers of glass or acrylic to help insulate the aircraft from the harsh outside climate, and they're actually larger than the window frame in the fuselage, so there's no way for them to pop out. The plasic window you can touch is actually part of the interior wall, and not the window itself. The small hole drilled near the bottom of the win-dow (which sometimes looks like a small metal cylinder) lets the air pressure equalize between the layers while minimizing the movement of air in the window. As the aircraft reaches cruise altitude, where the outside air is almost sixty degrees below zero (Fahrenheit), the moist air inside the airplane often crystalizes around this small hole. However, as the flight continues and the air inside the cabin dries out, the crystals usually evaporate.

Like water, air is actually slightly sticky. Just as ski racers wear very smooth clothes to reduce the amount of friction from the air, airplanes must have glassy-smooth exteriors in order to fly efficient-ly. Don't let how an airplane looks on the ground fool you; the air pressure inside the airplane at cruise altitude actually expands the fuselage slightly like a balloon so that it's taut. In fact, doors and windows are often inset a few millimeters from the fuselage so that they'll expand to be flush with the fuse-lage during flight.

Most airplanes that fly internationally have their home country's flag painted on or around their tails. Generally, the flag is fac-ing the proper way on the left (port) side and is painted backward on the right (starboard) side. Why backward? Because that's how it would look if a real flag were hoisted on a pole above the airplane during the flight.

AIRPLANE ENGINES

Pilots have a saying: "You could fly a barn door if you put a big enough engine on it." True, a powerful engine is often more important than an elegant wing design. However, in the real world, aircraft engines must not only provide a lot of power (forward thrust) but also be lightweight and fuel efficient. It's a tough challenge; in fact, the Wright brothers couldn't have succeeded ten years earlier than they did, simply because a suitable engine hadn't been invented yet. Sixty-five years later, the first Boeing 747s rolling off the assembly line looked great but couldn't fly because no aircraft engines on the market were powerful enough. (Fortunately, engine manufacturers caught up within a few months.)

The engines that drive propellers are more or less like automobile engines—they combust fuel to move piston heads, which turn a crankshaft, and so on. However, jet engines are totally different. In an airliner's jet engine, air is sucked in by a large rotating fan, then moved through a series of smaller and smaller fan blades, which compress the air down into a small chamber. These fan blades (there are more than 1,000 of them) must be precisely positioned; otherwise, when rotating at high speeds, they could cause an imbalance that could ultimately destroy the engine.

In the center of the engine, jet fuel is sprayed into the compressed air and then ignited. Unable to move out the front of the engine, the incredibly hot air expands and

How powerful are jet engines? In May 2000, a chartered jet carrying the New York Knicks basketball team taxied too close to a line of cars parked on the tarmac. The blast from the taxiing jet flipped head coach Jeff Van Gundy's car into the air and over three other cars, completely demolishing it.

shoots out the back, providing forward thrust. On its way out, this hot air moves through a series of small turbine blades, spinning them like windmills.

Commercial airliners built since the 1970s operate what are called *high-bypass jet engines*. In a high-bypass jet, the energy created by the turbine blades not only generates electricity to power the airplane but is also transferred through a shaft back to the front of the engine, where it spins a set of larger blades (the ones you can see from outside the airplane). These large blades are much bigger than the jet engine itself, and they act much like propellers. Surprisingly, the large fan blades create the majority of the forward thrust— not the "suck, squeeze, burn, and blow" action of the

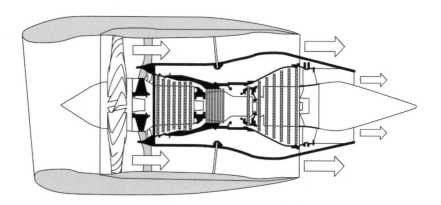

jet combustion chamber. Most of the air that is shot out the back of the engine actually flows over and around the turbine system—hence the name *high-bypass*.

Jet engines are very reliable because there are few moving parts. However, because the fans turn at such high speeds, it's crucial that they be extremely strong. When testing a new engine design, manufacturers strain it to the limits by shooting whole dead chickens into the moving fan blades at 180 mph (to simulate a bird getting sucked in at takeoff or landing), blasting torrents of water and ice into the engine, and even detonating dynamite inside it to ensure that broken fan blades won't pierce the engine's exterior shell.

How do you calculate an engine's horsepower? Horsepower is, by definition, based on velocity, so you can only describe horsepower at a particular speed. At takeoff speeds, (about 160 mph or 290 km/h) each pound of thrust is about 1/2 horsepower, so the 100,000 pounds of thrust from each engine on a Boeing 777 produce 50,000 horsepower, the equivalent of about 200 Porsches. At 375 mph, the horsepower is twice that (one pound of thrust equals about one horsepower at this speed).

Even if you strapped on giant wings, you could never fly because the human heart can't pump blood quickly enough to satisfy the enormous strain of flapping. When flying, a sparrow's heart pumps more than 450 times each minute!

The human arm provides pretty good thrust: The farthest a paper airplane has ever been thrown from the ground indoors is 193 feet (about twice the length of a basketball court), by Tony Feltch in 1985. Ken Blackburn holds the record for longest sustained flight by a paper airplane: 18.8 seconds. He had to throw the airplane 50 feet straight up in the air to accomplish this feat.

Each engine on a Boeing 777 can produce 115,000 pounds of thrust and is wider than the fuselage of a Boeing 727 (about eleven feet, or 3.4 meters, across).

A turboprop airplane is powered by a jet engine with a propeller in the front—the propeller is rotated by the turbines.

THE SOUND
BARRIER

People have been talking for years about the "sound barrier" as though it were a physical obstacle, like some invisible gate that had to be blasted through to achieve supersonic (beyond the speed of sound) flight. Of course, before 1947 no one had been able to travel faster than the speed of sound—airplanes would literally fall apart as they approached this "barrier"—but that was simply because scientists didn't yet understand the dynamics of high-speed flight. Today, military jets regularly surpass the speed of sound.

So why don't commercial passenger airplanes fly this fast? Because today the "sound barriers" are economic, environmental, and social. It is significantly more expensive to build and fly a supersonic airplane—some say as much as three times more than regular subsonic aircraft. For instance, the Concorde (the only commercial supersonic airline ever put into service) flies at twice the speed of sound, burns twice the amount of fuel per hour as a Boeing 747, but carries only 100 passengers and almost no cargo.

There is also some evidence that supersonic aircraft, which tend to fly at high altitudes, can damage the atmosphere's ozone layer. But one of the largest concerns is that supersonic aircraft create sonic booms, like window-rattling thunder, wherever they go. (It's a common misconception that these airplanes make a single boom as they pass the speed of sound. Not so; the sound is continuous, but people on the ground only hear the shock wave briefly after the airplane passes.)

Sound travels by molecules bouncing into one another. (When you talk, your vocal cords vibrate the air, and air molecules bounce all the way to your spouse's ear). The speed of sound is the speed at which these molecules bounce into one another, and it's called *Mach 1*, named after the man who first measured it, Ernst Mach (pronounced "mahk"; 1838–1916). It's about four times faster in water than in the air, and it's faster in hot air than in cold air. At sea level, Mach 1 is about 760 mph (661 knots, or 1,223 km/hr). However, it's colder at airline cruising altitudes, and Mach 1 is only about 665 mph (575 knots, or 1,068 km/hr).

A boat moving in water pushes some water ahead of it, and airplanes do the same thing with the air. However, at Mach 1 the airplane is moving at the same speed that the air molecules can push forward, and beyond Mach 1 (Mach 2 is twice the speed of sound), the airplane moves faster than the molecules can move. This creates a sharp shock wave where the air transitions from not moving at all to suddenly being very compressed, and the shock wave ripples out for many miles, like a wake behind a boat.

Unfortunately, as airplanes approach Mach 1, there is increased drag and they fly less efficiently. Today, almost all commercial airliners fly between Mach .80 and .86 (each airplane model has its own optimum speed). That's about 560 mph (485 knots, or 900 km/hr) at cruise altitude. Also, remember that air speeds up as it travels over the wing, so some parts of the wing may experience supersonic flight even when the rest of the airplane is below Mach 1.

The Concorde cruises at around 55,000 feet altitude at about Mach 2, over 110,000 feet (35,000 meters) per second. However, it takes off at only about 250 mph and lands at about 190 mph. During takeoff and landing, the aircraft's long pointed nose tilts down so that the pilots can see the runway.

The reason sonic booms sound like thunder is that a crack of thunder is actually a sonic boom created by lightning, which heats the air around it so fast that it expands faster than the speed of sound.

HOW FAST DOES
IT FLY?

The common housefly beats its wings up to 200 times per second to fly about 4 mph.

The woodcock is the world's slowest-flying bird, clocking in at about 5 mph.

The Wright brother's original airplane, the *Flyer,* flew about 10 mph, though a later model could fly up to 30 mph.

In 1979, cyclist Bryan Allen became the first pilot to fly across the English Channel using only human power. The seventy-pound aircraft, called the *Daedalus,* flew at about 18 mph.

The dragonfly has been around for about 250 million years and can fly 30 mph.

Blimps typically fly at about 35–40 mph. That's about the same speed at which flying fish glide through the air for up to 150 feet.

Boomerangs rotate about ten times per second at about 50 mph.

The Canada goose has a six-foot wingspan and can fly hundreds of miles at 60 mph.

Flying disks, like the Frisbee, aren't just toys. They can soar at 74 mph.

A hockey puck "flies" across the ice at 90 mph.

The *Voyager* was the first airplane to fly nonstop around the globe on a single load of fuel, cruising at 122 mph.

The popular Cessna Skylane private airplane cruises at about 170 mph, about the same speed as a fast-flying golf ball.

Many helicopters average only 60 or 70 mph, but a fast helicopter like the AH-64A "Apache" can fly up to 225 mph.

The peregrine falcon (*Falco peregrinus*) is the fastest animal on Earth: It can fly (in a dive) at 217 mph (about 90 meters per second).

The Gulfstream III executive jet can fly eight passengers and a crew of three at 509 mph.

The fastest propeller-driven aircraft is the "Rare Bear," a Grumman F8F2 Bear Cat that has flown at 528 mph.

The Boeing 747 has a cruise speed of about 580 mph.

The U.S. Air Force's F-86E "Sabre" flew at speeds up to 690 mph during the Korean War.

In 1947, Chuck Yeager broke the sound barrier for the first time, flying at Mach 1.06, about 697 mph, in a Bell X-1 nicknamed "Glamorous Glennis."

The Concorde flies at a cruising altitude of 55,000 feet (16,765 meters) at Mach 2, or 1,336 mph. It can fly 3,740 miles without refueling.

The McDonnell Douglas/Boeing F-15 "Eagle" can fly at about Mach 2.5, or 1,875 mph.

The comic book character Superman is said to fly faster than a speeding bullet. The bullet from a .38 Special "flies" only around 600 mph. However, the bullet from a .22 cartridge rifle exits the muzzle at about Mach 2.6, or 2,000 mph.

In 1974, the Lockheed SR-71 "Blackbird" set a transatlantic record by flying 3,470 miles from New York to London in just under two hours, and on July 28, 1976, it set a world speed record at Mach 3.2 (2,193 mph).

The fastest airplane ever flown was the X-15, which in 1967 reached Mach 6.7 (4,520 mph). It was able to fly as high as 354,200 feet, or 67 miles above the Earth.

The space shuttle reaches Mach 21 (about 18,000 mph) when it reenters the Earth's atmosphere. The friction of the air moving over its special protective tiles heats them up to more than 2,200°F.

THE GIMLI GLIDER

The next time you're at a party, ask your fellow guests: "What do you get when a jet airplane, flying at 41,000 feet, completely runs out of fuel?" Most people immediately picture an aircraft plummeting to the ground like a rock—after all, how can an airplane fly without fuel? Now tell them this story:

On July 23, 1983, Air Canada Flight 143 took off from Ottawa on its way to Edmonton. The two-engine Boeing 767 had no trouble flying to a cruise altitude of just over seven and a half miles in the sky. Suddenly, halfway through its journey, just after the passengers had finished their dinner, the left engine went out. Airplanes are designed to be able to fly with one engine inoperative, but the pilots decided to reduce altitude and were beginning to redirect the airplane to a closer airport when the second engine flamed out.

The airline later discovered that a series of bizarre errors by the pilots and ground crew, and computer malfunctions caused the airplane to be loaded with 9,144 kilograms of jet fuel—about half the amount required to reach their destination.

So what happens when all the engines go out? The jet airplane becomes a very large, very expensive glider. The 767 can glide about eleven miles forward for each mile it loses in altitude, but that still only afforded flight 143 about fifteen minutes in the air. Unfortunately, the onboard electronic and hydraulic equipment requires engine power, so the cockpit controls went dark and the flight instruments became very difficult to manage.

But remember that there are always multiple backup systems in an airplane. In this case, the 767 was fitted with a Ram Air Turbine (RAT), which uses a propeller to provide electrical power: The RAT automatically lowers from the belly of the airplane, and the wind rushing by turns the propeller, which runs a small generator. This system offered just enough hydraulic pressure to move the control surfaces on the wings and tail.

An aircraft built for gliding (soaring) typically has about a 60–to–1 glide ratio—it will glide 60 feet forward for each foot it descends. Most commercial jet aircraft have approximately a 15–to–1 glide ratio. That is, an airplane flying at 35,000 feet can glide about 525,000 feet (about 100 miles, or 160 km).

As the 767 glided over the vast Canadian heartland, the pilots calculated that the only airport within their range was the decomissioned Royal Canadian Air Force Base in Gimli, on the west shore of Lake Winnipeg. However, neither the pilots nor air traffic control knew that the airport's primary runway was now being used for auto racing. Worse, July 23 was the Winnipeg Sport Car Club's "family day," and dozens of parents had parked their cars and campers outside the edges of the runway to watch their children race go-carts on the straightaway.

Without engines, Flight 143 approached the airport silently, but even though it was dusk, people couldn't help but see the giant wide-body descending on them. Parents and children scattered in every direction as the 767 landed hard, blowing out two tires with explosive force. The main landing gear under the wings had dropped by gravity alone, as it was designed to do in an emergency, but the front gear hadn't locked into place, and the airplane's nose bulldozed the asphalt for more than 3,000 feet, trailing a 300-foot shower of sparks.

Amazingly, not one person on board or on the ground was injured as the airplane scraped to a stop. However, when the crew began the emergency evacuation, they discovered a slight problem: With the nose on the ground, the rear emergency slides dropped to

Remember that the space shuttle has no engines when it reenters the Earth's atmosphere. It doesn't drop straight down; it glides!

the ground at a near-vertical angle, and several people suffered injuries hitting the tarmac.

The Air Canada aircraft had sustained $1 million in damages but was able to fly out only two days after. In fact, the aircraft is still in use and will forever be known as the Gimli Glider.

Believe it or not, after the Gimli Glider landed, the Air Canada mechanics who were dispatched to drive to the airport and repair the aircraft ran out of fuel en route.

Many an elementary school pupil has confounded his or her classmates by declaring, "Scientists have *proved* that bumblebees can't fly." Indeed, scientists have long been mystified because the equations that describe how fixed-wing aircraft lift off the ground don't seem to work when applied to bugs. But, of course, *something* holds up these creatures, and the scheme appears to be similar to that used by airplanes. Birds, too, have similarities to airplanes, but as living flyers get smaller they rely on increasingly exotic aerodynamic tricks to wrest themselves into the air, and until very recently these tricks have eluded scientists' efforts to find them.

Bird Flight

Some aspects of bird flight mirror airplane flight almost exactly. In a glide, for example, a bird's wing acts just like an airplane's wing: a simple airfoil with a curved top producing lift by deflecting air downward. But where airplanes use engines to create forward thrust, birds flap their wings. The motion is complex, with the bird not only flapping but also twisting and folding its wing during part of the stroke. Scientists have tethered birds in wind tunnels, photographed them with high-speed motion picture cameras, and found that on the upstroke, wings rotate back and up,

A bird is an instrument working according to mathematical law.

—Leonardo da Vinci, 1505

with the leading edge on top and wingtip feathers open to decrease airflow resistance. On the downstroke, the leading edge rotates back down and the feathers close, acting as small airfoils, propelling the bird forward.

Birds also turn and twist their wings to maneuver, a process observed by the Wright brothers in their studies of pigeons. In fact, the Wrights modeled the steering mechanism in their first airplane after the twisting motion of a bird's wing. Soon after, aircraft were designed to roll with ailerons (those panels near the wingtips that can be raised or lowered), as these were much easier to engineer and construct than twistable wings.

Airplanes, like birds, widen their wings during slow flight, generating more lift in situations such as takeoff and landing. Also, the structures and internal systems of birds (at least of those that fly) are optimized for flight—built strong but light, like the best-designed aircraft. Airplane power systems run fast and hot, burning large quantities of fuel. Birds operate at higher body temperatures than other animals and have racing metabolisms. The metabolic screaming meemie of the bird world, the hummingbird, burns around 4 percent of its body weight per hour. A Boeing 747 burns around 3 percent per hour—over ten tons of fuel.

During migration, some birds can fly for distances rivaling the range of some airplanes. The ruby-throated hummingbird, which weighs about as much as a penny, flies nonstop over the Gulf of Mexico, a distance of 620 miles. That's nothing compared to the four-inch-long blackpoll warbler, which, in its autumn migration from Canada to South America, flies continuously for ninety hours without midair refueling, a feat that puts all airliners to shame.

Bug Flight

Insects, which first took to the air about 350 million years ago, were considered by early aerodynamicists to be more or less like tiny birds. But after aerodynamic calculations failed to account for enough lift, twentieth-century scientists tethered insects in wind tunnels and observed that many of them didn't flap their wings up and down like most birds. Instead, they generally flapped front to back, like a rower with an oar. Plus, aerodynamicists realized that air has a certain viscosity, and if you were the size of a bug, the air would seem thick. The smaller the creature, the thicker the air feels, so small insects like fruit flies can be thought of as swimming in molasses, rather than flying in air.

Even with this understanding of air viscosity, it wasn't clear how some insects could pull off the feat of flying. Models of insect flight using supercomputers failed to determine the missing lift sources, so scientists turned to dynamic scaling—constructing large working models of insect wings. The first breakthrough came in the mid-1990s from Charles Ellington, professor of zoology at the University of Cambridge in England. His lab constructed a large set of mechanical wings based on those of a gray hawkmoth. When the model was set to flapping in a wind tunnel with smoke streams, Ellington was able to observe a vortex—a spinning cylinder of air like a sideways tornado—above the leading edge of the wing.

Curiously, this type of vortex had been observed in wind tunnel tests of airplane wings, but always as a brief, unstable effect that occurred when the wing's angle of attack (the angle at which the wing meets the oncoming air) was

Insects flap their wings much more often than birds. Ruby-throated humming-birds click in at 70 beats per second, bees at 200 beats per second, and mosquitos at around 600 beats per second (600 Hz), which produces their irritating whine.

The bat is the only mammal capable of true flight.

increased to the point of stall (where the wing begins to lose lift). The vortex would appear at the airplane wing's leading edge and momentarily increase lift dramatically just before the stall. Ellington found that moths can do what airplanes can't: hang on the edge of a stall, taking advantage of the added lift of this leading edge vortex and, just before the vortex dissipates, quickly redirect and rotate their stroke to generate the same kind of lift with the wing going the opposite way.

Unfortunately, this added lift from the delayed stall might be sufficient to explain the aerodynamics of some larger insects, but it still can't account for the lift from tiny insect wings, which often flutter forward and backward like oars in a figure-eight pattern. Another solution was supplied by Michael Dickinson at the University of California, Berkeley. By immersing a giant set of Plexiglas fruit fly wings in two tons of mineral oil (which would model the relative thickness of the air that the fly swims in), Dickinson's lab discovered not one but two additional sources of lift exploited by the fruit fly. First, at the end of a wing stroke, the wing quickly rotates, and this flip mimics the backspin on a baseball—lowering the pressure on the top of the wing and generating a small amount of lift. Second, as the wing starts its backward stroke, it encounters the remains of the vortex shed from the previous stroke, which acts like a little headwind, generating even more lift with the faster airflow.

There are so many different kinds of insects (7,000 new species are found every year), with so many different types of wings, it may take some time before all their aerodynamic tricks are known. In the meantime this new understanding of microaerodynamics has led researchers to begin developing flying microrobots that might someday be used as ultraminiature spy planes.

Why do jet aircraft fly higher than the highest mountains? First, flying above the troposphere (the lowest layer of the atmosphere, where almost all bad weather can be found) offers a much smoother ride. Second, the higher the aircraft flies, the less dense the air, meaning less drag. On the other hand, thin air has less oxygen to feed jet engines, and fewer air molecules to maintain the airplane's lift. Plus, the less dense the air the slower the speed of sound, so flying too high forces pilots to fly slower. Each aircraft model has an optimum cruise level based on its design and the amount of fuel it carries. On long international flights, as heavy fuel slowly burns off, pilots will ascend to a higher cruise altitude every two or three hours.

In America there are two classes of travel: first class, and with children.

—Humorist Robert Benchley

If the Wright brothers were alive today Wilbur would have to fire Orville to reduce costs.

—Herb Kelleher, founder,
Southwest Airlines, 1994

The world's largest paper airplane had a wingspan of forty-five feet, ten inches. Built by students and faculty at Holland's Delft University of Technology in 1995, it flew (indoors) for 114 feet, six feet less than the Wright brothers' first powered flight.

THE SKYWAYS

Between departure and arrival, airplanes must contend with two important factors: the weather and air traffic control. Fortunately, while both the force of nature and the force of human regulation are somewhat mysterious to the passenger, they're relatively predictable to pilots. Using radar, computers, years of experience, and high-tech navigation and communications equipment, pilots and air traffic control guide airplanes through the clouds along invisible highways in the sky. The following chapters explore the weather, air traffic control, and one of the most important topics to all passengers: turbulence.

WEATHER

Weather affects almost every aspect of flying, but sometimes the effects aren't what you'd expect. For example, many people would say they prefer flying on warm, sunny days rather than cold, drizzly ones. But in reality, cool weather and light rain can provide less turbulent conditions than clear, hot, sunny days, when air can be more active or unstable.

And what about those big cotton-ball clouds that rise thousands of feet into the air like giant mushrooms? As harmless as they might seem from the outside, the turbulence inside these clouds (called *cumulonimbus*) can be so extreme that it can shake a plane like a bean in a child's rattle. This turbulence is caused by quickly rising warm air, which cools, falls, warms, and then rises again in a cycle. Moisture in the air condenses into rain, which freezes at high altitudes and then falls, only to be caught up in another column of rising air. Soon the ice crystals inside cumulonimbus clouds

The *troposphere* is the part of our atmosphere from the ground up to about six or seven miles (about 9.6 km)—it fluctuates depending on atmospheric conditions. At the top of the troposphere (where airplanes usually cruise), the temperature is usually around −58 degrees Fahrenheit (−50°C). Above the troposphere is the *stratosphere,* where the temperature actually rises again—to about 26 degrees Fahrenheit (about −3°C)—because the air at that altitude absorbs more ultraviolet radiation. What we experience as "weather" always occurs in the troposphere (though some large thunderheads sometimes break up into the stratosphere). In the stratosphere, the Sun is always shining.

can grow into hail as big as golf balls and can dent the wings or even crack windows of an airplane.

Cumulonimbus clouds can develop into thunderstorms, and pilots tend to avoid anything having to do with thunderstorms. In fact, commercial pilots might fly their planes through heavy rain and wind, but pilots will go to any lengths to avoid the core of a thunderstorm (the red areas on a weather radar). Don't get the wrong idea; it's unlikely that thunderstorms—or even hurricanes—would cause an airplane to crash, but they cause very expensive damage and incredible stress (to both the airplane and the passengers).

Storms also introduce three other important weather conditions: lightning, wind shear, and ice.

Lightning

Although you might think lightning would be one of the most destructive forces in the sky, the truth is that it has relatively little effect on airplanes. True, one airplane crashed because of lightning in the 1950s. However, since then all airplanes have been fitted with static wicks that dissipate electrical charges, and today lightning strikes an airplane somewhere almost every day without incident. The static wicks, fitted along the trailing edge of the wings and tail, draw off electrical charges that collect on the metal frame. So lightning might hit the airplane in the front and quickly dissipate out the back.

As a passenger, you don't have to worry because you cannot touch the metal exterior—you're completely insulated from the electricity. Lightning could make a direct strike on the fuselage, and the passen-

One of the strangest forms of lightning is *ball lightning,* which can form inside an airplane and appear to be rolling down the aisle while glowing and sparkling. Ball lightning is so rare that scientists haven't been able to study it to explain why it happens. Although it's startling, it has never harmed anyone.

gers would notice nothing more than a loud bang.

Nevertheless, the airplane doesn't escape completely unscathed. A bolt of lightning momentarily heats the air around it to about 50,000°F (about 7,600° C)—hotter than the surface of the Sun—often burning a small hole in the metal skin of the plane, which simply gets patched at the next mechanical inspection. Lightning might destroy an antenna, but that's one reason why airplanes have more than one.

Wind Shear

Sometimes it's what's invisible that counts: Wind shear occurs when an airplane travels through air that is blowing in two different directions or speeds within a small area. Wind shear happens frequently at all altitudes—it's actually one of the main causes of turbulence, and it's very rarely dangerous. However, when wind shear is severe and occurs at low altitudes, it can be hazardous to airplanes taking off and landing.

Here's why: Let's say a plane is landing at an airport when suddenly it encounters a strong headwind. The airplane gets more lift from the air traveling faster over the wing, so the pilot needs to slow the plane down and bring it to a lower altitude to maintain its path. Then, if the airplane suddenly comes upon a mass of air that is moving in the opposite direction, the headwind becomes a tailwind, the air flowing over the wings slows dramatically, and the aircraft quickly loses altitude. If this happens at several thousand feet, the pilot can quickly regain control, but if it's within a few hundred feet of landing, the aircraft could fly into the ground.

This sort of severe low-altitude wind shear happens during *microbursts* of air that sometime develop under thunderstorms. A microburst is like water pouring out of a faucet into a bathtub filled with water; the air blasts down, hits the ground, spreads out, and bounces back up again. The whole microburst might be only a mile wide and last fifteen or twenty minutes (probably only five minutes of which it's particularly strong). Some low-altitude microbursts are even strong enough to damage trees and buildings on the ground.

> When flying over a thick blanket of clouds, you can occasionally spot long stripes, like lines drawn in the sand. This is usually caused by large rivers because the cold water makes the air directly above them descend instead of rise.

The good news is that these sorts of microbursts are relatively rare around airports. Also, detection has become easier with Doppler radar (on the ground) and wind shear detection devices (in cockpits), and pilots are better trained to avoid and handle wind shear than ever before. Although there were several wind shear crashes in the 1960s and 1970s, training and early detection have meant almost none since 1985.

Snow and Ice

Airplanes can lift hundreds of thousands of pounds into the air not just because they have wings but because the wings are a very specific shape. If the shape of the wing changes even a little bit, the airplane isn't as efficient and requires more power to keep aloft. That's why airliners are so sensitive to ice forming on the wings. In some cases, just a half-inch (12 mm) of ice along a wing's leading edge can reduce its lifting power by 50 percent.

So before a plane takes off in a snowstorm, the airport ground crew must spray the wings with a deicing fluid to keep snow and ice off them until it's airborn. If takeoff is delayed for some reason, the aircraft may have to be deiced again

> One of the most fascinating natural wonders in the air is called the *glory*: a rainbowlike light that sometimes surrounds the shadow of the airplane in or on the tops of clouds. Glories are caused by diffraction of light in the cloud's water droplets (the larger the water droplets, the smaller the glory). Actually, the center of the glory isn't the airplane; it's where *you're* sitting in the airplane.

while it waits, just in case. Fortunately, once a jet airplane is in flight, heat from the engines is circulated through the wings to keep them ice-free. Smaller, propeller-driven planes often don't have this heating system and so are more susceptible to the dangers of ice when airborne.

In-flight deicing isn't just used for flying through storms. At high altitudes, the air is so cold that water vapor instantly turns from gas to ice as soon as it has something to latch on to (like a wing or even tiny particles in the engine exhaust). Pilots may not be able to see the full length of the wings from the cockpit, but they generally turn on the heaters as soon as they see ice begin to build up on the windshield wipers.

By the way, snowstorms produce concerns on the ground as well as in the air. A half-inch snowfall doesn't sound like much, but over a 10,000-foot runway it means clearing thousands of cubic feet of snow. Mounds of snow along the sides of a runway can't be too high, or else they might catch a wingtip as the airplane taxis to the gate. Also, the glycol- and urea-based fluids that airports use to deice airplanes and runways become toxic to fish and plants if they're carried into nearby lakes and rivers by snow runoff. Some airports have specially designed drainage systems or wastewater treatment plants just for this purpose.

Flying Forecasts

Pilots are keenly aware of weather conditions at all times, and they won't even take off if it isn't safe. Besides, there are strict rules regarding what pilots may and may not do in every sort of weather condition, so any inconsistency in the pilots' personal judgment is not an issue.

During a flight, pilots constantly monitor the onboard weather radar so they can avoid areas of heavy precipitation or anything that even looks like a thunderstorm. Each airline also employs a team of meteorologists who forecast the weather around the clock in order to minimize flight delays and other problems. If the need arises, the airline can even radio special weather reports to the pilots. (Many pilots insist that these weather forecasters are among the great unsung heroes of the aviation industry.)

One of the trickiest conditions to forecast is fog, which is just very low cloud cover. Back in 1945—long before modern warning systems were the norm—a U.S. Air Force bomber pilot became disoriented in the fog above New York City and crashed into the seventy-ninth floor of the Empire State Building, blasting a twenty-foot hole in the side of the building and killing all three crew members plus eleven people in the building.

Today, flying through fog isn't a problem, but when it comes to taking off and landing, each airport and each airplane are rated for a minimum allowable visibility (the distance you can see the runway and other objects clearly). Some airports also impose a minimum ceiling (the distance of clear air from ground to clouds), often about 200 feet. However, some experienced pilots with special training and some aircraft with special equipment are allowed to land in low-visibility and low-ceiling situations.

Believe it or not, some newer aircraft (like the Boeing 777) and pilots are even rated to land in virtually zero-visibility conditions based on electronic instruments that are installed at some airports and on the airplane. In these cases, the autopilot can do everything from land to taxi to park outside the gate.

Ultimately, as scary as harsh weather can seem when flying, it's extremely rare for weather conditions to be the cause of an accident in this day and age.

TURBULENCE

"Did you have a good flight?"

You can hear this question uttered thousands of times each day by friends and relations greeting passengers at airport gates, but if you listen carefully you'll find that what is really being asked is: "Was there much turbulence on the flight?"

For most people, a good flight means a smooth flight, and there's nothing like bad turbulence to make passengers swear they'll never fly again (though a screaming baby in the next row is a close second). Even relatively calm fliers tend to find themselves glancing nervously around when an airplane starts bouncing and shaking through the sky. After all, how much turbulence can an airplane take?

Rating Turbulence

Pilots have four ratings for turbulence: light, moderate, severe, and extreme. If you have a glass of water in front of you during a flight and you can see surface ripples, you're in light turbulence. If the water starts sloshing around but doesn't spill out of the glass, you're in moderate turbulence. It's not until the glass is literally flying above your tray and the water is in your lap that you're in severe turbulence. (By the way, if the bumps are steady and rhythmic rather than irregular, pilots call it *chop* instead of turbulence.)

Everyone knows someone who claims to have been in *extreme* turbulence, "so bad I thought for sure I was going to die." However, the truth is that few people—even pilots who have been flying for thirty years—have ever experienced extreme turbulence. In fact, over 99 percent of the turbulence people feel on commercial airplanes is only light or moderate chop (even when it feels like it must be severe or extreme).

One reason for this is that strict rules prohibit U.S. airlines from flying into an airspace where there is known severe or extreme turbulence—like the center of a thunderstorm or a hurricane. Airplanes *can* fly into extreme turbulence and survive (the government frequently sends military or research pilots into hurricanes to measure wind speed), but since it's almost impossible that you'll find yourself in that situation, assume that the rest of this chapter deals only with light to severe turbulence.

What Is Turbulence?

What pilots know but most passengers don't is that airplanes fly just as capably in the midst of turbulence as in smooth, calm air. Turbulence doesn't make the pilots panic or clutch the controls in a desperate effort to control the plane. Turbulence doesn't tear wings off commercial airplanes or shake the fuselage apart.

Flying through turbulent air is much the same as steering a powerboat across choppy water. In a boat, passengers expect the thud-thud-thud of the water hitting the bottom of the boat, the rising and falling seesaw of the boat's hull, and the sometimes unexpected drops. Just as boats are strong enough to survive the impact of turbulent water, airplanes are built to withstand turbulent air.

In fact, some pilots who fly their own private airplanes on their days off actually look for turbulent air because it's fun to fly through. However, pilots on the job try to avoid turbulence simply because they know the passengers don't like it.

To understand what turbulence is, you have to understand that air is just like fluid. Remember: Just because you can't see the air doesn't mean it's not there. Once you can visualize that airplanes are moving through a really light "liquid," it's easy to see what causes turbulence.

First, some parts of the air are warmer than others (like the air above parking lots on a hot day), and the hot parts rise because they're less dense. As hot air rises, it pushes the cold air down. The lava lamp, that icon of the 1960s, is a pretty good visual representation of exactly this effect. Or imagine a fish swimming through an aquarium while you pour water into it: Some of the water is moving down, causing other parts of the water to rise up, and the fish gets a bumpy ride.

Now imagine the wind blowing over a mountain range: The air hits the mountain and gets pushed up, just as water in a stream is pushed over rocks. But the air above the mountains pushes the wind back down—the result is a wave of air moving up and down, also called a *mountain wave*. This can be surprisingly uncomfortable and is no fun to fly through. Fortunately, it is a well-understood phenomenon and easily forecast, so pilots can typically fly around it.

Another cause of turbulence is the "wake" from other airplanes. Just as a boat moving through water causes a wake, an airplane leaves a trail of turbulence in the air. However, the bigger the airplane and the slower it's flying, the bigger the ripple. Small airplanes have to be very careful about flying behind large jets because they can literally be flipped over by the spiraling vortices trailing off the bigger aircraft's wings. Fortunately, pilots and air traffic control keep this in mind and schedule plenty of space between airplanes.

High Winds and Turbulence

High winds don't always cause turbulence; in fact, airplanes enjoy smooth flights in the middle of the jet stream, where winds can be blowing at over 200 mph. While small airplanes (which carry between two and ten passengers) can be blown around by strong gusts of winds—causing a sensation of rising, falling, and sliding from side to side—it's rare for larger jet airliners to be affected by wind speed alone.

The turbulence you feel on these aircraft is typically due to changes in wind-speed or direction. That is, if the wind is blowing in one direction in one part of the sky and in a different direction elsewhere, then the boundary between the two areas will be filled with swirling eddies (just like water when two rivers converge). This is sure to cause a little turbulence because the airplane will experience slightly less lift over the wing, then more lift, then less lift, and so on until it passes through the boundary into the new, stable wind condition.

If the eddies are large and slow-moving, the turbulence may feel like driving over speed bumps slowly. If they're tight and swirling quickly, it might feel like driving over those small, reflecting lane dividers on a road. Sometimes one wing gets slightly more lift than the other, and the airplane tips to one side and then the other quickly; again, this just means that the wings are hitting different parts of the airflow.

It's also important to note that in most cases, turbulence doesn't make the whole aircraft ascend or descend. Rather, when passengers in the front of the airplane feel a slight upward motion, the passengers in the rear feel the equivalent downward motion. Even a small change in pitch—where the nose moves up or down by three inches—can feel surprisingly strong when it occurs quickly. This is why seats near the wings (the fulcrum of the seesaw) often provide the smoothest ride.

The Air-Pocket Fallacy

Sometimes when you're flying, you experience the sensation that the airplane is dropping. Many people—even professionals—call this *hitting an air pocket*. It's a terrible feeling—as if suddenly there is nothing holding the airplane up—and you could swear it dropped hundreds or thousands of feet in a split second. However, the reality makes for a much less interesting story.

There is no such thing as an air pocket—that is, airplanes can't fly into a bubble where there's no air any more than a boat can hit a "pocket of no water" in the middle of a lake. When you drive over a big pothole in the road, your car's wheel may actually lose contact with the road for a moment as it drops, but there is no way for this to happen in an airplane.

Yes, the airplane may descend very quickly for a short time, but it is still surrounded by air. Often the "drop" happens when the aircraft flies into a column of rapidly descending cold air (a *downdraft*); other times the aircraft flies into an area where the wind direction is radically different. In either case, the airplane always moves through the offending air quickly, often following the short descent with a rapid ascent. Again, this is analogous to a motorboat cresting over a wave and dropping suddenly, only to be raised up on the next wave. It might feel and even sound as if the airplane is bouncing hard against something, but airplanes aren't damaged any more than boats are.

Remember that our bodies are easily fooled in airplanes, and although we might feel like we're dropping hundreds of feet, the reality is that airplanes just don't do this. Pilots can watch the airplane's altitude change on the cockpit's altimeter, and they know that usually these sudden motions are only a matter of a few feet—maybe as much as twenty or fifty feet, but that's not a big deal when you're cruising six miles (9.6 km) up.

You Can't Escape Turbulence

No passenger wants to fly through choppy air, but insisting on flying without turbulence is like expecting the water to be perfectly calm whenever you're on a boat—it just isn't going to happen. The important thing to remember is that as long as you've got a seatbelt on, air turbulence is not a safety issue; it's just a comfort issue.

The people who are hurt in those very rare severe-turbulence situations are the folks who are walking around, like flight attendants. That's why if there's any chance of moderate or severe turbulence, the pilots ask the flight attendants (and everyone else) to be seated.

Flying in good weather is no guarantee of a smooth flight (*clear air turbulence*—or *CAT*—can happen even on a beautiful sunny day), but there are a few things you can do to minimize your discomfort. First, flights in the morning are often smoother than those later in the day, when the air has had a chance to warm up. Second, when turbulence tilts the front of the airplane up a little, the back usually goes down, and vice versa. Therefore, you can sometimes reduce the feeling of rising and falling by sitting near the middle of the airplane.

Remember that pilots and air traffic controllers are constantly working to avoid turbulence. When an airplane encounters some, it slows down and air traffic controllers try to assign it an altitude where the air might be more stable. They also redirect any aircraft that might be heading toward the rough air.

AIR TRAFFIC CONTROL

Most airline passengers are aware that pilots are in communication with air traffic control (ATC) throughout each flight. United Airlines even allows passengers to listen in on this communications channel on some flights, though it can be difficult to understand the staccato bursts of coded language from pilot to controller and back again. In many ways air traffic controllers are the backbone of the airline industry—ensuring the safety of passengers and in-flight aircraft at all times—but who, and where, are they? Probably the best way to understand the air traffic control system is to follow a single typical flight.

From Gate to Gate

Before the pilots push back from the gate, they must get permission from ground control, which is stationed in the airport's control tower. Ground controllers keep watch over the gates and taxiways around an airport, using their eyesight (often with binoculars) and, at larger airports, ground radar to tell them exactly where every truck, cart, and aircraft is around the airport. As the airplane heads toward the runway, ground control hands the pilots over to tower control, also located in the airport tower, which oversees the runways, managing the precise timing of takeoffs and landings.

This kind of "hand off" from one air traffic controller to another is key to the whole system. A controller gives the pilots a radio frequency, like 121.83 (in megahertz), and one of the pilots dials it into one of several radios on the instrument panel. Then the pilot flicks a switch from the old frequency to the new one, so the pilots are never stuck "between channels." Once on the new frequency, the pilots listen for a lull in the new channel's communication in order to introduce themselves to the new controller by stating their airline, flight number, and location—for example, "Delta 486, approaching runway 11R." The controller confirms recognition, in this case by repeating "Delta 486 . . .," and then provides further instructions.

> If you have a window seat on an airplane, you'll notice that the wings are typically bright silver while on the ground and a darker blue–gray when at cruising altitude. That's because the metal wings are reflecting diffuse, scattered light while on the ground. In the air, the light isn't as scattered by dust and water vapor, so we see a better reflection of the dark blue sky above.

After tower control gives the pilots permission to take off, and once the aircraft is in the sky, tower control hands the pilots off to Terminal Radar Approach Control (TRACON), which handles all air traffic within about thirty miles of the airport. The TRACON controllers supervise all arrivals and departures for one or more airports. For example, the TRACON in Oakland, California, manages traffic into and out of three major airports in close proximity—in San Francisco, San Jose, and Oakland—plus a handful of smaller airports, like those in Hayward and Palo Alto. There are about 185 TRACONs spread out across the United States, each based at or near an airport.

However, the TRACON controllers only oversee air traffic up to an altitude of 17,000 feet, so the pilots are only in communication with TRACON for a matter of minutes before they're handed off to an Air Route Traffic Control Center (ARTCC, or just Center), which handles all high-altitude flights en route to their destinations.

> The windows in an airport control tower must always be tilted out at exactly fifteen degrees from the vertical to minimize reflections both inside and outside the control cab.

In a small country, there may be only one Center

controlling all the traffic. In Canada, there are seven Centers: in Vancouver, Edmonton, Winnipeg, Toronto, Montreal, Moncton, and Gander. In the United States, there are twenty-one: in Albuquerque, Anchorage, Atlanta, Boston, Chicago, Cleveland, Denver, Fort Worth, Houston, Indianapolis, Jacksonville, Kansas City, Los Angeles, Memphis, Miami, Minneapolis, New York, Oakland, Salt Lake City, Seattle, and Washington, D.C. Because a single ARTCC may oversee several states and hundreds of thousands of square miles, each Center is broken into sectors, typically between 50 and 200 miles wide. Each air traffic controller at a Center (which is usually a windowless building nowhere even near an airport) is assigned a sector to manage, and as an aircraft travels from one sector to another, the pilots are handed off from one sector controller to the next, and (on long flights) from one Center to the next.

The system is much the same on international flights. When flying from New York to London, for example, the pilots are passed from New York to Gander Ocean Control (in Newfoundland, Canada) to Shanwick Ocean Control (which is actually located in two cities: Shannon, Ireland, and Prestwick, Scotland).

Finally, when the aircraft is approaching its destination, the sector controller leads the pilots down to a lower altitude and then hands them off to the destination airport's TRACON arrival controller, who lines up each incoming aircraft properly before handing the pilots off to a tower controller. Once on the ground, the pilots are handed off to the local ground controller, who directs them through the taxiways to the proper gate.

Keeping the Distance

About 50,000 airplanes fly over the United States each day, from private single-engine aircraft out for joyrides, to "puddle jumpers" flying commuters over short distances, to jumbo jets on intercontinental flights. Air traffic controllers must constantly be aware of where each airplane is, as well as where it is headed, so that no two airplanes get too close to each other. They obtain this information primarily through the use of radar, sophisticated computer software, and information received from each airplane's *transponder* (a device that responds to radar signals by transmitting a code back that identifies the particular aircraft, its position, and its current altitude).

Air traffic control laws are complex, but they can be boiled down to a few rules.

> Radar can be compared to a flashlight shining into the night sky: When the light hits something, like a bird flying by, it bounces back into your eyes so you can see it. Radar uses light waves that the eye can't see; if the radar beam hits an object, it bounces back (echoes) where it can be picked up by a sensor. Light waves travel so fast that the whole process happens in less than one hundredth of a second.

▼ Takeoffs and landings generally need to be separated by at least two minutes, though this interval is extended after the takeoff of "heavy" aircraft, such as a wide-body Boeing 777, so that subsequent aircraft won't get caught in wake turbulence.

▼ Near an airport, aircraft must be separated by three miles (in good weather) or five miles (in bad weather). At higher altitudes, aircraft are kept at least ten or twenty nautical miles apart (or even more, in poor weather).

▼ However, when flying over areas of the world that don't have en route radar systems—such as the Atlantic and Pacific Oceans, inner Australia, and much of Africa—pilots must maintain ten or fifteen minutes' flying time between themselves and other aircraft. At cruise speeds, that means between 80 and 140 miles apart, when they're at the same altitude.

▼ Below 29,000 feet, aircraft must maintain a 1,000-foot (305 meter) vertical separation. Older altimeters (instruments that measure altitude) are less accurate at great heights, so above 29,000 feet, aircraft need 2,000 feet (.6 km) of vertical separation. Newer systems are far more accurate, and the rules are slowly changing to accommodate the higher number of airplanes in some areas.

▼ Above 18,000 feet, pilots and ATC discuss altitude in terms of *flight level*. Flight level 210 (FL210) is 21,000 feet, FL320 is 32,000 feet, and so on.

▼ Below flight level 290, eastbound aircraft (those traveling between 0 and 179 degrees on the compass, where 0 is due north) fly at odd-numbered altitudes, such as FL230. Westbound aircraft fly at even-numbered elevations, such as flight level 240. However, above FL290—at typical cruising altitudes for large jets—all flights are set to alternating odd-numbered altitudes, with eastbound aircraft flying at FL290, 330, and 370, and westbound flights at FL310, 350, 390, and so on.

Of course, there are always exceptions to these rules, and different countries have slightly different regulations. For example, both China and Russia use the metric system for speeds and altitudes.

Old Systems, New Systems

Air traffic control has been the focus of a lot of concern around the world, and especially in the United States, where much of the equipment used would be considered obsolete in any other industry. Yet because of the enormity of safety issues involved in air travel, change happens extremely slowly. Nevertheless, in the years to come, old-fashioned radar screens will increasingly be replaced by computer screens fed by satellite-based Global Positioning System (GPS) information, and communication among various con-

Hang gliders and other unpowered aircraft in the United States can legally fly up to an altitude of 17,999 feet in powerful updrafts of air. Technically, they could fly even higher, but all aircraft at 18,000 feet or higher must be regulated by the federal air traffic control.

trollers and airlines will likely become much easier.

Air traffic control is already becoming increasingly computerized, as software tools at traffic controller's fingertips make it possible to manage more aircraft than ever before in busy airspaces, such as those around Chicago and over the North Atlantic. Some researchers today believe that future air traffic controllers will work in computer-generated, three-dimensional environments, complete with virtual-reality goggles and gloves, where they could "fly" through the airspace and see a complex matrix of aircraft from any angle.

Commercial pilots who fly on international flights and the flight controllers whom the pilots talk to are required to be able to speak English, the international language of flight. When a French airline travels to Germany, all air traffic communication is handled in English. However, pilots making domestic flights within their own countries sometimes speak with the controllers in their own language.

Airplanes often cruise at around 35,000 feet. That sounds like it's pretty far up, but compare this altitude to the size of the Earth itself: If the Earth were shrunk down to the size of a typical desktop globe, the airplane would be cruising at only one-tenth of an inch (2.5 mm) off the surface.

Note that when you're flying at cruising altitude, the stars don't appear to twinkle—the lights on the ground do. The twinkling is caused by heat and particles in the lower atmosphere.

The larger the airplane, and the slower it is flying, the more powerful its wingtip vortices. If you stand below a jumbo jet when it lands, you may even hear a flapping sound and see ribbons of water vapor, both created by the wingtip vortex.

FROM POINT A TO POINT B

In theory, the shortest distance between two points is always a straight line, but figuring out the shortest distance between two airports isn't so simple. Airplanes almost never travel in straight lines from place to place (except on very short flights). Rather, they take a route based on legal restrictions, optimum fuel efficiency, and shortest time in flight.

For example, it's obvious that the fastest way to travel from San Francisco to Tokyo is directly west, over the Pacific Ocean, right? Not so. Using a string and a globe, you can see that the shortest distance is to fly north toward Alaska, then west toward Russia. You're still flying in more or less a straight line, but it's over the curvature of the Earth, so the path appears bowed on a map. In general, the farther east or west you need to travel, the closer to the poles you'll fly.

Legal Restrictions

Sometimes airlines are forbidden to use the shortest path because of sensitive geographic politics. North American aircraft have to get special permission to fly over countries such as China and Russia. And even domestically, they're prohibited from flying too close to nuclear power plants, military installations, and other "no fly" zones.

All U.S. and Canadian airlines (as well as those of most other countries) have to follow another important legal restriction: Two-engine aircraft must remain within a designated amount of flying time from an airport, in case an engine fails. These aircraft are designed to fly just fine at a lower cruising altitude with just one engine, but no one wants to take a chance that the other engine might fail, too. The rule used to be 60 minutes from an airport, but in 1985 the Federal Aviation Administration (FAA) instituted the ETOPS (Extended Twin-engine Operations) program, which specified that these aircraft could fly up to 120 minutes from an airport, as long as the airline followed more strict maintenance and operations guidelines.

> [Flying across the American Midwest] is really one of the odd sights of the world, and it is strictly an air sight: a whole country laid out in a mathematical gridwork, in sections one mile square each; exact, straight-sided, lined up in endless lanes that run precisely—and I mean precisely—North-South and East-West. It makes the country look like a giant real-estate development; which it is. One section has 640 acres. A quarter section, 160 acres, is the historical homestead.
>
> —Wolfgang Langewiesche, A FLIER'S WORLD

The difference between 60 minutes and 120 minutes was dramatic: Before 1985, almost every trans-Atlantic flight was on a four-engine aircraft, like the Boeing 747, because a twin-engine would have to follow a circuitous route that was far from fuel-efficient.

In 1989, based on extensive studies of the integrity and durability of modern jet engines, the FAA extended the ETOPS limit to 180 minutes. This allowed airlines to fly twin-engine aircraft almost anywhere in the world, including Hawaii. In the year 2000, the FAA extended it even farther, letting some Boeing 777s fly 207 minutes from an airport, which permits even more direct routing between the United States and Asia. Today, the majority of flights across the North Atlantic are flown on the twin-engine Boeing 767.

Of course, the ETOPS limits still don't allow for the most efficient routes on some international flights. For example, flights between the United States and Japan still have to hug the coast of Alaska a bit more than airlines would like.

> In the near future, the FAA may raise the ETOPS limit for some aircraft to 240 minutes. One likely result of this decision would be the closure of some very remote airports—such as the one in the Midway Islands in the Pacific Ocean—which are kept open at great cost by the aviation industry for the sole purpose of extremely rare emergency landings.

Weather

Many people don't realize that the same flight may use a different route each day. The reason? The weather.

Each airline has its own team of meteorologists who forecast the weather and help figure out the best routes to fly. Of course, commercial airplanes always avoid the centers of thunderstorms or clouds of volcanic ash, which can sometimes make for indirect routes. But airplanes may also fly seemingly odd routes in order to avoid or get closer to jet streams, which are very powerful high-altitude winds that blow from west to east (in both the northern and southern hemispheres), especially during the winter months. Streams can be 100 miles wide and 2 miles from top to bottom, often blowing at more than 150 mph (130 knots) at the center.

A jet stream moving at this speed would either add or reduce 150 mph from a plane's air speed, depending on whether the aircraft is heading east or west. That is why it often takes about an hour longer to fly to the United States from Europe than the other way around. So, each day, airlines and government officials adjust the long-distance flight routes, directing eastbound airplanes into the jet stream, and westward flights out of it.

Sky Highways

Navigation and air traffic control also keep airplanes from flying in straight lines from departure to destination. In the early days of aviation, pilots had to watch for landmarks on the ground to know where they were; sometimes airmail companies would even light bonfires on hilltops as beacons that their pilots could follow. It's not so different these days, except the beacons are radio transmitters sending out VOR (Very-high-frequency Omnidirectional Range) signals.

Before takeoff, the airline gives the pilots a flight plan detailing each point along their route. A 1,000-mile flight might include five VOR beacons, over which the airplane will fly as it makes its way in a relatively straight line from signal to signal. The paths between these beacons—often called corridors or highways in the air—are about nine miles wide and are clearly marked on aeronautical charts.

The Earth is spinning in space, and any given point on the equator is traveling eastward at over 1,000 mph (higher latitudes travel more slowly, as they have fewer miles to cover in the same amount of time). Fortunately, pilots never have to adjust for the rotation because the atmosphere spins at about the same rate. Wind speeds can make an even greater difference—an airplane flying eastward in the jet stream would be traveling at more than 1,700 mph (as seen from outer space).

For instance, a flight from San Francisco to Seattle would likely be "vectored" over four cities, each with a VOR station named with a three-letter code: Oakland (OAK), Red Bluff (RBL), Medford (OED), and Portland (PDX). Some VOR stations are in towns with small airports, and others are transmitters in the middle of nowhere set up by the government.

If your flight is running late, the pilots may ask air traffic control for a more direct flight, perhaps picking different VOR stations or even bypassing one or more beacons. This is increasingly possible due to Global Positioning System (GPS) technology that enables pilots to determine their exact location based on signals from satellites. In the future, GPS combined with longer-range airliners will make more direct paths possible, shortening flights and saving fuel and money.

From the air, the distinctions between residential, commercial, and industrial areas are easily understood while town, county, and state boundaries go unseen.

—Oliver Gillham, THE LIMITLESS CITY

✈ **air new zealand** *Boarding Pass*

Boarding Pass

TWA

FLIGHT
706

RETAIN THIS FOR RESERVATION A...

Please Note: Your seat has been specially rese...
please return to this seat before e...
inconvenience to yourself and fel...
on this flight have been released

SINGAPORE...
OR BOX...
18004...
SECURITY SCREEN...

FIRST CLASS

IN CABIN
BAGGAGE

Passenger Copy	Please be ready to board your flight no later than 15 minutes before departure time.	MUST be presented when boarding or reboarding.

FLIGHT	DESTINATION	SEAT
0770	LONDON	08-8
26AUG		FIRST

See Reverse Side
For Important Notice

SMOKING

K   FB   ORD   YES

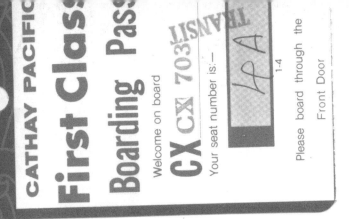

THINGS THAT GO BUMP IN THE FLIGHT

It's a natural human reflex to attempt to make sense of our experiences. So if you hear a series of loud noises, you'll wonder what caused them, and you're not likely to feel at ease until your imaginings are either confirmed or replaced with a more plausible explanation. Similarly, if someone tells you that you can't use your cell phone on an airplane but you're welcome to use the expensive built-in phone in front of you, your curiosity might naturally be piqued.

The next few chapters should help make sense of your experiences while flying—the bumps, the noises, and the announcements. Plus, there are some suggestions in case you experience anxiety or are concerned about your general health in airplanes.

BUMPS AND NOISES OF A TYPICAL FLIGHT

The next time you're a passenger in a car, try this experiment: Sit in the backseat and keep your eyes closed from the time the ignition is turned on until you're parked and the ignition is turned off. Of course, you probably won't actually be able to keep your eyes closed that long because the experience will be too disorienting and scary. When we can't see what's going on and why, every bump in the road is a surprise, every sound is magnified, and every sudden deceleration feels like impending doom.

Sound familiar? Even people who aren't fearful of flying often find the plethora of noises and bumps on an airplane mystifying, if not downright anxiety-provoking. It doesn't have to be that way, though.

If you could sit in the cockpit with the pilots, the source of most sounds would be immediately obvious ("Oh, I heard that *whump* sound because the pilot just retracted the landing gear"). Unfortunately, that isn't possible, so the rest of this chapter is devoted to explaining all of the things that go bump in the flight.

The Push Back

When you first step onto an airplane, it's often "plugged in" to the airport's power supply in order to run the lights, air-conditioning, and other electrical devices. However, depending on the airport and aircraft, sometimes the power comes from

"The flight time today is five hours in first class and twelve and a half in coach."

A cartoon originally published in the NEW YORKER, October 2, 2000.

the airplane's Auxiliary Power Unit (APU)—a small jet engine near the tail which may sound like a high-pitched whine.

As you take your seat, you may see cold air condensing as it enters the air-conditioning vents inside the plane, especially on hot and muggy days; don't worry, it's not smoke! And the clunking and thumping you hear is just the crew wheeling food into the galleys and loading cargo into bays in the belly of the airplane. Sometimes the cargo rolls forward and hits the stops at one end or the other, shaking the whole plane a bit. The cargo doors are large and are typically closed by an electric motor, so they whir and thump.

Then, when everyone is boarded and seated, the flight attendants close and arm the doors (if the doors

When the lead plane gets the signal to go, and begins to gather speed, it looks to me like some-body's idea of a joke, as if you and I decided we could get a mobile home airborne if we could just get it rolling fast enough. I think a plane's first few moments off the ground look almost as untenable from the ground as they feel from inside.

—*Layne Ridley,* WHITE KNUCKLES

As the airplane lifts off the ground, your body momentarily becomes heavier (it's one of those wacky laws of physics). This force is measured in Gs (for *gravity*). At 1.1 G your weight is 10 percent greater than normal. You can easily see this effect if you carry a postal scale on board with you and weigh something during takeoff. Or try the following experiment: Put two paper clips on a thin rubber band; attach one to the seat in front of you and the other to something heavy. Upon takeoff, the heavy object gets heavier and pulls down on the rubber band.

are opened before they're de-armed, the emergency slides shoot out and inflate). Next, after another flight attendant double-checks that the doors are armed, they announce "cross-check complete" and the pilots can start to back away from the gate.

Of all the mysterious things that happen during a flight, one of the strangest occurs just as the engines are starting up: The air-conditioning stops, and the lights in the cabin blink out for a moment. In fact, this can happen up to four times before all the engines are going. These flashes of power seem more like brownouts and can give the impression that the whole airplane is malfunctioning. However, the power lapse actually occurs because the pilots must switch the electrical current from the APU (or the airport's power supply) to the generators in the main engines.

When the power comes back on, a bell sometimes dings, and if you listen carefully, you can hear the jet engines start to turn with a low hum (usually first on the left wing and then the right).

Airplanes almost always take off into the wind. While it seems like a headwind would slow them down, in fact the speed of the aircraft isn't important at takeoff; it's the speed of the air over the wings that is crucial. If there's a 20–mph head–wind and the airplane is moving at 100 mph, the relative airspeed is 120 mph. But if the airplane flew with the wind instead, the airspeed would only be 80 mph.

The pilots don't always start the engines while you're still sitting at the gate. The airplane may be silently pushed back to the taxiway by a truck (a *really* powerful tow truck), or it may "power back" with its thrust reversers. The latter can be surprisingly loud, as the engines must rev up and blow a lot of air to move the heavy aircraft.

On the Taxiway

At peak travel times, when airplanes are backed up waiting to take off, you may spend a lot of time taxiing to the runway—plenty of time to listen to the sounds around you. It's not uncommon to smell a burning, acrid smoke while taxiing. The good news is that you're not smelling your own airplane burning; the bad news is that you're smelling the exhaust from the airplanes in front of you. Fortunately, it passes as soon as you're in the air.

As the aircraft rolls steadily toward the runway, you'll hear bump, bump, bump as the wheels run over lights or metal expansion joints embedded in the pavement. The brakes often squeal and whine when the airplane slows or stops; this does not mean they're failing! Airbus aircraft feature a Power Transfer Unit (PTU)—it transfers power from one engine to another—which unfortunately sounds like an electric drill mounted on the bottom of the fuselage, between the wings. You may hear this startling noise a few times before takeoff and again when taxiing to the gate after landing.

Then, somewhere along the ride to the runway, the pilots extend the wing's flaps and leading edge slats to assist in takeoff. If you're sitting near the wings, you'll likely hear the whirring noise of gears and a metal screw turning, sometimes surprisingly loudly. When air traffic control gives the pilots permission to take off, the pilots first alert the flight attendants with a brief announcement and then push the engine throttles forward.

There are few things on Earth that seem as improbable as a jet airplane taking off—whether you're watching it or sitting inside of it. The engines suddenly get very loud, and the bumps from the wheels quicken. Occasionally, depending on wind and runway conditions, the whole aircraft starts to shake, and items in the galleys that were meant to be fastened down fall over with clattering bangs. Sometimes it sounds and feels as if the pilots are straining the jet to its limits and the whole aircraft could fall apart at any minute. This is only an illusion—airplanes have more than enough power to take off and are far stronger and more flexible than they appear.

First Moments of Flight

At last the pilots tilt the nose of the airplane up, increasing the angle at which the wings approach the air, and the aircraft gains enough lift to take off. As the wheels leave the ground, you may hear a dull thud as they extend to the end of their struts. Suddenly, the airplane seems to climb rapidly—at what may feel like a forty-five-degree angle, but the maximum allowed is twenty degrees, and the average is only fifteen degrees.

Occasionally, air traffic control instructs the pilots to turn almost immediately after takeoff (for noise control or simply to get the airplane heading in the right direction). This, too, may feel extreme (as though the airplane were banking at forty or even sixty degrees); however, the maximum turning angle allowed is thirty degrees, and pilots rarely turn more than twenty or twenty-five degrees.

Next, the pilots raise the landing gear in order to streamline the airplane. You'll hear a clunking sound in the belly of the fuselage as the wheels are raised and the landing gear door closes (if you're sitting over the landing gear, it may even sound and feel like a car running over a small branch on the road). Remember that those wheels are spinning at over 100 mph when you leave the ground, so the brakes are automatically applied, which can also cause a bit of vibration during the first moments of flight.

Then, seemingly for no reason, you'll hear the engines lower in pitch and volume, and the airplane seems to slow down and perhaps even drop in altitude. This doesn't happen on every flight, but when it does you might think that something is wrong. It's not; the pilots reduce power and level off a bit because of noise abatement guidelines or air traffic control's altitude restrictions. The airplane is actually still increasing in speed and altitude, but our bodies are extremely sensitive to *changes* in acceleration. It's like when a car enters a freeway—after the initial boost of speed, it's very difficult to get a sense of how fast you're moving.

Now those flaps that were extended before takeoff in order to maximize the lifting power of the wings are no longer needed, and the pilots retract them (with the same sort of whirring noises). This may happen two or three times, as they're usually retracted in small increments.

Cruising Bings and Bongs

For all the high-tech gadgets and brilliantly designed features on the modern jet airplane, the system the crew uses to communicate with one another is surprisingly simple: bells or chimes. You'll hear bings or bongs sporadically throughout the flight: When a flight attendant in the front of the airplane wants someone in the back to pick up the intercom phone, he or she will signal with one or two chimes. When the pilot is ready for a cup of coffee, you'll hear a chime (usually a slightly different tone). When a passenger presses the call button, you'll hear a chime, too. (Worse, when a small child finds this button, you may hear a series of chimes.)

The pilots also use chimes to signal that the airplane has climbed above 10,000 feet, and some airlines signal again when the airplane passes through 18,000 feet. When the seatbelt light goes on or off, it's accompanied by a chime. Also, in some aircraft, the chimes are accompanied by colored lights at the front and back of the cabin: one light means a call button was pressed in one of the lavatories, a second one indicates a crew-to-crew message, and a third light means a passenger call. The one thing a chime does *not* signal is that there's an emergency, so you don't have to be concerned about chimes.

While the aircraft is cruising, the only other sound you typically hear is the engine noise (which is louder at the back of the airplane) and the sound of air moving over the skin of the airplane (which is much louder than you'd expect).

The Approach

As the airplane approaches its destination, the ride seems to get a little quieter (though by then your ears are so used to the background roar that it's hard to tell). This is because the pilots have reduced the engine power considerably, and the airplane is probably just gliding down at idle power toward the airport, much like taking your foot off the gas pedal on a highway exit ramp. Then, as the airplane slows, the pilots extend the wing flaps once again. Birds do the same thing: As a bird lands, it spreads its feathers out to gain better lift at slow speeds.

You'll likely hear another chime as the airplane passes down through 10,000 feet (this isn't automatic; the pilot has to flick a switch, so it's rarely at exactly this altitude), and the pilots lower the landing gear around 2,000 feet, with the corresponding mechanical clunks and thuds.

If you have a view of the wings, you can usually see the big metal flaps on top of the wings, called *spoilers*, being raised a little during the approach. Spoilers make the airplane lose altitude and slow down, but they can also cause some choppy vibrations.

Finally, as the airplane is almost touching down on the runway, you'll often hear a sudden rise in the pitch and volume of the engines. Pilots sometimes increase the throttle while making small last-minute adjustments for as smooth a landing as possible.

Landing

A *go-around* or *missed approach*—in which the airplane either lands and then immediately takes off again or doesn't even touch down before pulling up and circling around for another approach—can scare even the most seasoned passenger. However, go-arounds are more common than you might think, and they are almost never a sign of an emergency. There are reports of pilots going around because of a sudden unexpected gust of wind, a stray deer on the runway, or even just because something doesn't "feel right." It's important to remember that a go-around is not a last-ditch maneuver; the pilots discuss the potential for a go-around before every landing, and air traffic control reserves airspace for go-arounds, just in case.

Nevertheless, most passengers breathe a sigh of relief when the wheels finally touch down, the spoilers on the wings pop up, and the reverse thrusters kick in. These thrusters don't actually shoot air out of the front of the jet engine, as one might think. Air still gets sucked in, but it is then deflected forward by metal panels that block the path of the exhaust stream (either inside or behind the engine itself). However, while the reverse thrusters help the airplane slow down, airplanes can stop even without them. The wheel brakes alone are so powerful that a loaded 747 can stop in as few as 3,500 feet, absorbing as much kinetic energy as a million automobile brakes.

As the airplane rolls down the runway it's very common to hear a thumping, which can sound like one of the landing gear tires has blown out and is flapping around. Actually, the sound is simply the result of the pilots landing right in the center of the runway, and the wheels are running over the runway centerline lights. Some pilots try to land slightly off center to avoid this distracting noise.

Finally, as the "fasten seat belt" sign is turned off at the gate (with another chime, of course), you may see the lights flash off and on again, as the airplane's power supply is switched from the engines to the gate power (or the APU). The flight is over; now it's time to tackle the really scary part of the trip: the airport and the drive into town.

THE TROUBLE WITH CELL PHONES

There are two kinds of people in the world: those who are content to leaf through a magazine or book while waiting for takeoff, and those who get itchy when their cell phone, pager, laptop computer, and handheld digital datebook aren't turned on and within easy reach. Unfortunately for this second group, the airlines and the Federal Aviation Administration have instituted rules restricting the use of these sorts of electronic "vices" on airplanes.

Currently, gadgets that intentionally emit signals—such as cell phones and wireless e-mail and Web surfing tools—are totally prohibited from the time the airplane leaves the departure gate until it arrives at its destination gate (called "from block to block" in the trade). Other electronic tools—such as laptops, CD players, and handheld games—are banned until the aircraft reaches 10,000 feet.

Some technology lovers complain because airlines prohibit their favorite toys but allow electronic devices such as heart pacemakers, electric shavers, voice recorders, and hearing aids. This is not a minor issue; there are reports that the ban on cell phones is now the second largest cause of "air rage," after alcohol.

The problem is simple: *All* electronic devices emit electromagnetic radiation, and those emissions can possibly interfere with the airplane's sensitive electronics (like the navigation equipment, which is partly based on radio transmissions). That's just the nature of electronics. When you turn on a digital calculator, it creates a very weak electromagnetic signal. When you turn on a radio, it creates a stronger one. A cell phone emits a lot of signals, even when you're not talking on it. This is why many hospitals ban cell phones from areas with critical health-monitoring devices.

Electromagnetic radiation is like light (in fact, what we call visible light is actually a form of electromagnetic radiation), so imagine that your laptop computer is emitting a blue light and the airplane's radio transmitter is emitting and receiving a red light. If you happen to be sitting near an antenna (which is on the outside of the airplane), your blue light could contaminate the red light a little, causing signals to and from the airplane to be less clear than they should be.

Why the 10,000-foot rule? Because the airspace around airports and cities is already lit up with an astonishing amount of electromagnetic radiation, and the airlines figure it's better not to add to the jumble. Plus, pilots would have more time to deal with any interference at higher altitudes than they would closer to the ground.

Unfortunately, there is no proof that laptops or even cell phones actually do cause any significant problems. A number of airline pilots have provided anecdotal evidence (like the time a pilot realized that whenever a particular passenger turned on his laptop, the aircraft's compass would deviate ten degrees off course), but no one has been able to scientifically repeat the interference in experiments. Perhaps the problem only occurs rarely, based on the electromagnetic radiation in the air on a given day. As the FAA's Thomas McSweeny noted, "We are preventing the extremely remote event."

The U.S. Federal Communications Commission (FCC) also bans the use of cell phones in flight, but for a completely different reason. When you use a cell phone on the ground, your phone typically receives and transmits signals with only one antenna station at a time—whichever is currently within direct line of sight. From the air, your phone could communicate with dozens or hundreds of antennae, which could (in theory) disrupt communications for cell phone users on the ground, according to the FCC and cell phone companies. The onboard phones, which are often expensive for passengers to use, work on a completely different antenna system than regular cell phones and are shielded in order to avoid any radio interference.

TIPS FOR ANXIOUS FLIERS

About one out of every three people feel some anxiety when flying, so if you're one of them you're not alone! However, the majority of anxious fliers aren't actually afraid of flying; they just don't like the emotions and sensations they feel when they fly. This is why safety statistics don't usually make anxious fliers feel any better. "I know all that," they reply, "but I still don't enjoy flying." Plus, the more airlines make flying feel like riding a crowded bus, the less comfortable people feel and the faster their anxiety increases.

Of course, there are lots of reasons that people get nervous in airplanes. Some folks are afraid of being stuck in a closed space (claustrophobic), and others are afraid of heights (acrophobic)—though ironically, many acrophobes have no trouble flying or even skydiving because there's so little frame of reference that far up.

But for the most part, nervous fliers suffer from two things: the feeling of not being in control and not understanding how or why airplanes work. This isn't surprising: you *aren't* in control when flying as a passenger. But not being in control of the aircraft doesn't mean you're "out of control," and it doesn't mean you're not safe. You are still in control of yourself and how you react to your environment. And you're still very safe. Most people think they're in control when driving, and yet about 300 times more people die on the roads in North America than in airplane crashes. Remember: You can't rely on your anxiety level (or how much adrenaline is pumping in your bloodstream) to tell you how much danger you're in.

Often, people—particularly women—develop flying anxieties between ages twenty-five and thirty-five, and especially after a major event such as the birth of a child or a parent's death. It's also very common for people to become anxious about flying after a scary experience such as significant turbulence or a go-around (when the airplane is about to land but suddenly takes off again). These unexpected events can be really frightening if you don't know that they're almost never actually dangerous. Of course, terrorism or airline disasters, such as the hijackings in September 2001, tend to confirm people's worst fears of not being in control, though they hardly affect overall airline safety.

Remember that fear intensifies around the unknown and the unseen. Studies have shown repeatedly that the more you know about airplanes and flying, the more comfortable a flier you'll be. (See The Fear Factor, pages 115–38)

Learning what is and isn't dangerous is the key to flying confidently. For example, the fact that air is invisible is at the root of many people's anxiety. Some people are nervous about the aircraft's doors opening while in flight, and they are surprised to learn that this isn't physically possible (because the door is actually wider than the door frame, and the air pressure inside the airplane is greater than it is outside).

A surprising number of people avoid flying in propeller airplanes and go out of their way to fly on jet aircraft, believing them to be safer. However, in the 1950s and 1960s, the situation was just the opposite, and airlines had to work to convince passengers that jet engines were safe, even though you couldn't see what was pro-

> When I was just starting out, my folks used to travel with me on tour. My mom was petrified of flying, so she went to the doctor and he prescribed pills to help calm her. She took one before getting on a plane and another when we were in the air. By the time we landed, she was very relaxed. How relaxed? I turned around and she was sitting on the conveyor belt! She rolled right out in front of the customs officer. It was like a scene straight out of I Love Lucy.
> —Singer Barbara Mandrell

> The world is divided into two kinds of people: normal, intelligent, sensitive people with some breadth of imagination, and people who aren't the least bit afraid of flying.
> —Layne Ridley, White Knuckles

> I am not afraid of crashing; my secret is . . . just before we hit the ground, I jump as high as I can.
> —Comic Bill Cosby

pelling the airplane forward. Today, when it comes to scheduled passenger airline flights, both propellers and jets are about equally safe. (Of course, this statistic doesn't include those small bush airplanes that fly in remote mountainous areas.)

What You Can Do

If you're prone to anxiety when flying, keep these suggestions in mind:

▼ Avoid caffeine in sodas, coffee, tea, and chocolate before and during the flight. It increases your heart rate and blood pressure. Also, avoid alcohol or other drugs. Although you may think that a drink will calm you down, it can actually increase anxiety because you feel less in control.

▼ Eat a healthy meal before you fly. Your body will feel better if you feed it well.

▼ Try to get a window or aisle seat near the front of the airplane, which often psychologically feels less confined.

▼ Arrive at the airport extra early. It's much better to read a magazine (or this book) at the gate than to stress about making the flight.

▼ Tell the flight attendants that you're a little anxious about the flight. They'll often take extra care to explain unexpected-but-normal events on the loudspeaker.

▼ If something scared you during your flight, don't disembark until you find out (from a pilot or a flight attendant) what really happened.

▼ Bring relaxing things on the airplane with you: music, a familiar scarf or picture you can pin to the seat in front of you, or some calming essential oils you can rub on your sleeve and sniff occasionally. You're going to sit there for a while, so make the space "your own."

However, if you have a more serious fear of flying, it's probably worth looking into a professional program. Many of these programs have an 85 or 90 percent success rate with fearful fliers. For a list of organizations that offer such programs, see *The Flying Book* Web site (www.theflyingbook.com).

STAYING HEALTHY IN THE AIR

Almost nothing can live in the incredibly harsh environment 6.5 miles (10 km) above the surface of the Earth, where there is little oxygen and the average temperature is -56°F (-49°C). Nevertheless, that's exactly where millions of people travel in airplanes each day. It's no wonder that many passengers feel terrible after getting off an airplane.

People routinely blame their icky post-airplane feelings on jet lag, airplane food, catching a cold from fellow passengers, or even "stuffy airplane air." However, the truth is that you *can* fly for long distances and walk off the airplane feeling reasonably good; it's not that hard if you follow the tips in this chapter.

Airplane Air

For an airplane to carry passengers tens of thousands of feet up, it must be pumped full of air (*pressurized*), like a sealed balloon, so that the oxygen is dense enough for passengers to breathe comfortably. But the more pressurized the airplane, the more strain on the fuselage, so airlines and governments have compromised: The air inside an airplane should be no thinner than the air at an altitude of 6,000 or 7,000 feet (about 2,100 meters). This rule is pretty reasonable—many mountain ski resorts are at even higher altitudes—but the air at this altitude can still affect passengers.

For instance, if you take off from an airport near sea level, the oxygen level of your blood will drop somewhat while you're flying. Although a lower oxygen level isn't dangerous for most people, it does make alcohol more potent, and you may feel dizzy or uncoordinated even without drinking any alcoholic beverages. Plus, some passengers, such as those with lung, heart, and blood conditions, may have trouble breathing without supplementary oxygen.

Actually, airplanes aren't entirely like "sealed balloons," because the air in the cabin is constantly being refreshed. Throughout a flight, hot air passing through the jet engines gets diverted through air-conditioning units (called *air packs*) and then mixed with recirculated cabin air and fed back into the cabin. Contrary to popular belief, this recirculated air is far from "dirty." In fact, modern airplanes use air filters similar to those used in hospitals, which can catch airborne microbes like bacteria and viruses.

To maintain a constant pressure as air is pumped in, the airplane has a pressure valve which lets some air out. The result is a complete fresh air change in the cabin every five or ten minutes—much faster than in most office buildings and even faster than in many hospital rooms.

The Earth's atmosphere filters out radiation from cosmic rays and the Sun, and the higher you fly the less is filtered out. Should frequent fliers worry? Most doctors believe that 50 mSv (milli–Sieverts, a measure of radiation dose) per year is a reasonably healthy upper limit, and the average person gets a dose of about 3 mSv from natural sources on Earth. A five–hour flight boosts your radiation dose by only about .025 milli–Sieverts. That means you could fly every day of the year, twenty–four hours a day, and still be fine. The one exception is pregnant women: Occasional flights won't harm a fetus, but pregnant pilots and flight attendants should be careful.

Ear Pressure

When you fly, the first sense that the air pressure is changing is probably a feeling somewhere in your inner ear. This is because the air that is trapped inside your

Air pressure in airplanes is serious business. If the cabin depressurizes while you are at cruise altitude and you don't put on an oxygen mask, you can become unconscious within thirty seconds. In such an emergency, pilots will always immediately descend to a safe altitude; if they didn't, anyone not wearing a mask could die within minutes.

Sure, you can catch a cold or flu from the passenger in the seat next to you, but it's extremely unlikely that you'd catch something from someone several rows away because the cabin air is filtered and changed so often. In fact, the air quality is as good as or better than it is in other forms of public transportation.

Air expands as the airplane lifts into the sky. That's why you shouldn't fly for two or three days after extensive surgery or dental work: Tiny air bubbles trapped in your teeth could expand and be very painful. Similarly, don't fly for twelve hours after you scuba dive because air "trapped" in your blood and gas trapped in your bowels could expand.

body—including the little pocket of air behind each eardrum—expands as the airplane rises and the pressure drops. The expanding air presses against the ear drum, which can be uncomfortable. The same thing happens in reverse when landing: Air pushes in on the eardrum as the pressure rises.

Fortunately, the inner ear is connected to the back of the throat by the eustachian tube, through which air can escape. Unfortunately, this tube has no muscles of its own to keep it open, so it's usually in a collapsed state. Chewing gum, yawning, blowing up a balloon, making funny faces, and swallowing are all ways to get the eustachian tube to open for a moment so that the air can equalize on both sides of the eardrum, which we hear as a "pop." Another method, called the *Valsalva technique,* is to close your mouth, pinch your nose, and blow gently against your closed nostrils.

Not only are colds, sinus infections, and allergies associated with fluids and swelling that stop your eustachian tubes from opening, but they also trap air in the sinus cavities behind your forehead and cheeks, which can be excruciating. If you're congested like this, you should probably take a nonprescription decongestant a half-hour before takeoff. Of course, if the flight is a long one, you'll need to take another before the descent and landing. Some people have found EarPlanes ear plugs useful, as they slow the change in pressure against the eardrums.

This ear pain can be really unpleasant for infants and small children who don't know what's happening to them. Drinking from a bottle or nursing can help. A crying baby can be annoying, but remember that crying actually helps the baby open its eustachian tubes. One remedy for ear pain (your child's or your own) is to put hot, wet paper towels in the bottom of two cups and then hold the cups against the ears. The warm steam soothes the eardrums, but make sure no hot water gets into the ears!

> Even though airliners carry medical kits and can quickly be in radio contact with doctors on the ground, about 100 people die each year while flying, from heart attacks, seizures, or other medical emergencies.

General Health

While it's nice to have fresh air coming from outside the airplane, the problem is that air at high altitudes is extremely dry and it doesn't take very long before people become somewhat dehydrated. Add to that the general stress put on the body from a lower-pressure environment, a lack of sleep, a change in diet, and the stress of flying in general (getting to the flight on time, and so on)—it's no wonder that a passenger can feel poorly stepping off the airplane. Here are some tips that should help:

▼ Drink eight ounces of water for each hour you're in the air so you don't get dehydrated.

▼ Avoid alcohol, caffeine (in coffee, tea, Coke, Pepsi, chocolate, and so on), salty beverages (like tomato juice), and salty foods (pretzels, peanuts, and pretty much anything else that comes in a small snack bag). All of these items are dehydrating.

▼ Rub moisturizer on your hands and face before takeoff, and reapply in the middle of a long flight to counteract dehydration.

▼ Eat a healthy snack or meal before flying. Some studies show that drinking an electrolyte-rich "sports drink" before takeoff helps the body recover from flying faster. Bring some food on board with you, too; it'll likely be more pleasant than what the airline offers.

▼ Wear noise-cancellation headphones while in flight. These headphones can remove much of the ambient roaring noise that causes drowsiness and discomfort.

▼ The in-flight air may dry out your eyes and your sinuses, so wear glasses instead of contact lenses, and on long flights keep your sinuses moist with a sinus spray.

▼ Human bodies were not designed to sit in the same place for a long period of time. Get up and stretch once an hour (walk around, too, if the person next to you isn't snoring into his or her pillow). Plus, when sitting, don't cross your legs; it restricts circulation. Try to stretch a little before landing, too, so your muscles are warmed up before you have to stand up and walk.

▼ Get a good night's sleep before your flight. This not only makes you feel better but helps your body resist anything infectious that you might be exposed to.

▼ If you often feel ill on airplanes, you might be suffering from motion sickness. One solution is to sit by the window, where you can see the horizon or a cloud or anything that's not moving.

▼ Try to avoid touching your nose, eyes, and mouth while flying to help prevent viruses from entering your system. Also, wash your hands before traveling and regularly throughout a long flight, just in case you do touch your eyes or mouth without thinking. And don't visit the lavatory in bare feet or wearing only socks (don't laugh; a surprising number of people do this).

You may have heard of *economy class syndrome,* another name for *deep vein thrombosis (DVT)*. It's a potentially deadly disorder in which blood clots form in veins and deep within muscle tissue. DVT can strike anyone who sits in the same place for too long, whether flying economy class or first class, or even on a train or bus. One study showed that between 100 and 150 passengers arriving in Tokyo's Narita airport are treated for it each year.

With that in mind, it's very important to get up and move around on long flights (anything more than an hour or two). There are also many exercises that you can do in your seat. Walking up and down the aisles is great exercise.

Ankle circles: Lift your feet off the floor and draw circles with your toes, rotating your ankles. Repeat for about fifteen seconds, and then reverse direction.

Knee lifts: Raise each leg six or eight inches, bending the knee. Repeat twenty or thirty times per leg.

Shoulder roll: Rotate your shoulders in a circle by hunching forward, then raising shoulders, then gently pulling them back, then dropping them down. Repeat five times.

Arm stretch: Raise both arms as high above your head as possible (ignore the people behind you). Use one hand to gently pull the opposite wrist for about ten seconds. Then repeat using the opposite hand.

Neck roll: Relax your shoulders and drop your head forward gently. Roll your head to the left and hold about five seconds, then roll forward and to the right about five seconds. Repeat four times.

FLIGHT ATTENDANTS

Flight attendants have been serving passengers for almost as long as passenger flight has been in existence. The job's description has changed dramatically over the years, but it always comes down to the comfort and safety of the airline passengers. Britain's Daimler Airways was the first to employ dapper young men for the job, whom they called *cabin boys,* in 1922. In fact, it was strictly men-only until 1930, when Ellen Church talked her way into a job with Boeing Air Transport (a precursor to United Airlines). Her argument was simple: Most of the passengers were businessmen, and most of them were afraid to fly. (After all, air travel was still a very new phenomenon.) Having a woman on board would not only be a comfort but also instill a sense of confidence—if a woman could fly, then so could these men. Besides, Church was a registered nurse, which could come in handy in an emergency.

By the end of the year, Boeing had hired eight *stewardesses,* and soon other airlines were copying the idea. Applicants had to be nurses, unmarried, under twenty-five years old, and less than five feet four inches (1.63 meters) tall. The job wasn't glamorous in the late 1920s and early 1930s. Responsibilities included weighing passengers and their baggage, making sure the wicker seats were bolted down, shining shoes, swatting flies, and stopping passengers from throwing lit cigarettes out of windows or opening the exit door when they were looking for the toilet. At the end of a long day, the stewardess would even help push the airplane back into the hangar.

Still, the image of beautiful and cosmopolitan women on airplanes was a hit, and by the 1950s the airlines were using marketing slogans such as "Today's stewardess, tomorrow's wife." The requirement to be a nurse was dropped during World War II, but other demands were made: weight restrictions, and even wearing girdles, white underwear, and particular shades of nail polish.

By the late-1960s, however, the wholesome "sky girl" had transformed into a glamorous sex symbol used to sell tickets. Airline commercials featured stewardesses in hot pants purring slogans, such as: "Hi, I'm Rose and I'm going to fly you like you've never been flown before"; "Service just means having things around you that make you happy . . . Like me"; "We really move our tail for you"; and "Fly me, I'm Cheryl."

But this "Coffee, Tea, or Me?" fantasy image overshadowed the real role of the flight attendant: safety. Although most passengers still believe that 80 percent of a flight attendant's job is providing comfort, the truth is that they're there primarily in case of an emergency. Far from being cushy, the job requires extensive training (usually six to eight weeks plus a yearly review and updates), often grueling hours, and significant physical stamina (those carts they push around weigh about 250 pounds). And ironically, the one thing they're best trained to handle is the one thing most of them will never have to deal with: disasters.

Air travel has this hangover from the '50s and '60s where it was really glamorous and sort of elitist. Not anyone could just buy a ticket on Priceline.com for 60 bucks. You had to plan it, you dressed up and it was a big occasion. The reality is a lot different from what we have in our minds.

—Rene Foss, second-generation flight attendant, author of the musical revue AROUND THE WORLD IN A BAD MOOD

The specific rules regarding flight attendants vary among airlines and between countries. On Canadian airlines there must be at least one flight attendant for each forty passengers on the aircraft.

Don't mess with the flight attendants: Attacking them or interfering with their job is a federal offense.

After years of immortalizing historic characters, Madame Tussaud's Wax Museum in London decided to create figures of famous commercial occupations. The first commercial figure it created was a flight attendant: the world-famous "Singapore Girl" of Singapore Airlines.

Lawsuits brought about some major changes in hiring practices in the 1970s. Airlines in the United States began to hire men and drop some age and weight limits. In the following decades, the changing economics of flying forced fewer flight attendants to oversee more passengers, and their job became increasingly important and difficult. These men and women must constantly juggle their duel roles as both authority figures and reassuring, accommodating attendants. (Even their uniforms are a mix of military and vogue fashions.)

For all the work, a flight attendant's salary is nothing to write home about, especially in the first few years, and many of them work second jobs when they're not on duty. Plus, they cannot choose their flights or fellow crew members until they have gained seniority at their airline. That's one reason the flight attendants are often older on international and transcontinental flights—routes that are usually more desirable—than those on short domestic hops. Nevertheless, the perquisites of the job are great: Flight attendants can fly nearly free to anywhere in the world if there's an open seat on an airplane, and because they are often on call or on the job for days at a stretch, they often get three- or four-day "weekends."

ANNOUNCEMENTS REPORTEDLY HEARD ON VARIOUS AIRLINES:

"Your seat cushions can be used for flotation, and in the event of an emergency water landing, please take them with our compliments."

"We do feature a smoking section on this flight; if you must smoke, contact a member of the flight crew and we will escort you to the wing of the airplane."

"As you exit the plane, please make sure to gather all of your belongings. Anything left behind will be distributed evenly among the flight attendants. Please do not leave children or spouses."

"Weather at our destination is fifty degrees with some broken clouds, but they'll try to have them fixed before we arrive. Thank you, and remember, nobody loves you, or your money, more than [our] airline."

"Folks, we have reached our cruising altitude now, so I am going to switch the seat belt sign off. Feel free to move about as you wish, but please stay inside the plane till we land . . . it's a bit cold outside, and if you walk on the wings it affects the flight pattern."

© John Grimes, www.grimescartoons.com

In the 1960s, the now-defunct Braniff Airlines called flight attendants *hosties* and dressed them in eye-popping outfits designed by fashion designer Emilio Pucci. The uniforms were so reminiscent of something a James Bond girl might wear that the stewardesses came to be known as *Puccis Galore.*

CATHAY PACIFIC

First Class

Boarding Pass

Welcome on board

CX **CX** 703

TRANSIT

Your seat number is:—

1-4

Please board through the Front Door

Destination

☐ Non smoker

ية
اليمنية

Yem

Yeme

ARDI

gate

✦NAC BOARDING PASS
PLEASE PRESENT TO HOSTESS

FLIGHT	TO	SEAT
463	CHC	13F
		GROUP

This boarding pass is invalid unless attached to ticket.	EMPLANE

T.29

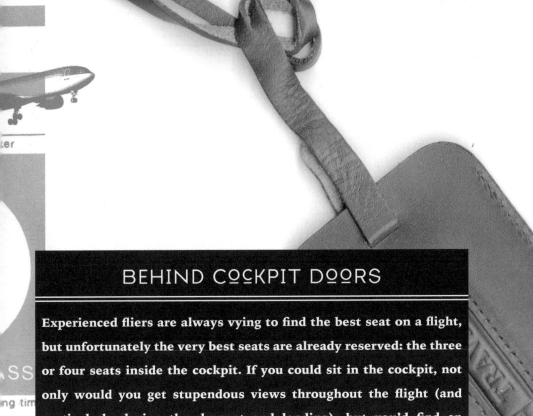

BEHIND COCKPIT DOORS

Experienced fliers are always vying to find the best seat on a flight, but unfortunately the very best seats are already reserved: the three or four seats inside the cockpit. If you could sit in the cockpit, not only would you get stupendous views throughout the flight (and particularly during the descent and landing), but you'd find an answer to almost every question about flying you might have. How can the pilots possibly manage all those cockpit instruments? Why is it so important that they know how heavy the airplane is? How do they tell the difference between all the runways at a big airport? And who are those pilots, anyway? The following chapters explore these questions, and more.

WHAT ARE THOSE PILOTS UP TO?

How many times have you boarded an airplane in a rush, settled yourself into your seat, and then sat and wondered: "Who's flying this thing?" It's rare to get more than a quick glimpse at the pilots, and yet we all want some kind of reassurance that they know what they're doing. That little speech they give about ten minutes after takeoff doesn't help. Even if it's not drowned out by airplane noise, the passengers are left thinking: "Was that voice old enough to fly this thing? Did it sound confident enough?" And while you sit, hurtling across the sky, what exactly are those pilots doing behind that closed door?

Although flight attendants are often rushing people to board and sit down as quickly as possible these days, it's a great idea to take your child up to the cockpit to meet the pilots before takeoff (or borrow someone else's kid if you don't have one and you're embarrassed to go up alone). Even if you just stick your head in and say, "Howdy!" you'll feel better having seen the pilots in their element. Don't feel bad if they can't talk long; they've got a lot to do before takeoff.

Who's in Charge?

Every passenger flight (other than tiny charter or commuter flights) has at least two people in the cockpit, the captain and the first officer. Some folks say "pilot and copilot," but that's not really correct, because they're both qualified pilots. In fact, the first officer might even have more flying experience than the captain, but perhaps not as many years with that particular airline—the positions are based almost entirely on seniority.

You can tell the difference between the two pretty easily: The captain sits in the left seat, has four shoulder stripes, and a laurel insignia on the brim of his or her cap. The first officer has only three stripes and no cap insignia. In older Boeing 727 and 747 aircraft, as well as in the DC-10, there is a third certified pilot in the cockpit: a second officer or flight engineer who monitors the airplane's hydraulic systems, air-conditioning, and other things that are handled entirely by computers in all newer airplanes.

While some pilots may look young, remember that they have typically flown for ten or twelve years, accumulating over 2,000 hours of flying time for cargo companies, the military, or small commuter airlines—before a major airline will even consider hiring them. Then, in order to get their *type rating*, the pilots must undergo intensive training on the particular type of aircraft they're going to fly, including practicing every sort of imaginable emergency situation in a flight simulator. Imagine if you had the chance to practice skidding your car in a snowstorm or handling it when the brakes go out . . . over and over until you mastered it. Pilots who have experienced potentially disastrous problems in flight report that they didn't panic—they just did what they had already practiced dozens of times in the simulator.

Some other interesting pilot facts:

▼ Pilots are typically certified to fly only one kind of aircraft at a time. A Boeing 747 pilot isn't allowed to fly a 727, even if she used to fly one. Of course, there are a few exceptions, such as several Airbus models that have almost identical cockpits.

▼ Pilots have to retire at age sixty (or even fifty-five in some countries). It's not really a safety issue, and many older pilots want to change this rule, but without forced retirement younger pilots would advance much slower.

▼ Captains must get a medical exam every six months, and first officers are required to have at least one each year. They both have an EKG at age thirty-five, and then annually after they turn forty. Also, both must have twenty-twenty vision, but they can wear contact lenses or glasses to achieve it.

▼ A pilot's *domicile* is the place from which his or her flights usually originate. However, the domicile isn't necessarily where the pilot lives. A pilot might live in California and be domiciled 1,000 miles away in Washington state. That pilot would have to commute to work by *jump-seating* on other flights (taking an available seat in the cabin or one of the extra seats in the cockpit).

▼ Airlines require their pilots to take additional training and testing each year. Often, these training sessions are designed to advance a 737 first officer to a 737 captain, or a 737 captain to a 757 first officer, and so on. Again, imagine how safe a driver you would be if you were required to take driver's education and testing every year!

▼ Although there's a public perception that pilots can be daredevils (think of the movie *Top Gun*), commercial pilots tend to be very conservative and cautious. Airlines don't want pilots who will take risks with their passengers and $200-million airplanes.

▼ Pilots typically aren't allowed to have beards. It's not a style issue; a beard would stop the oxygen mask from fitting tightly enough if the cabin pressure dropped suddenly. By the way, if one pilot gets up to use the toilet in the middle of the flight, the other pilot must put his oxygen mask on, just in case the pressure drops while he or she is alone in the cockpit.

▼ Pilots almost always have someone looking over their shoulder—literally! They watch each other in the cockpit, and airlines and regulatory organizations (like the Federal Aviation Administration) randomly perform *line checks* in which an inspector sits in the cockpit to review how well the pilots maintain proper procedures. Plus, cockpit computers and air traffic control are constantly monitoring what pilots do. Some pilots say it's like driving with a police car behind you all the time. There is also a surprising amount of paperwork they are required to file.

▼ While the FAA says that pilots cannot drink alcohol within eight hours of takeoff, many airlines have even stricter rules and won't let pilots drink a full twenty-four hours before a flight.

▼ You may have noticed that pilots carry or wheel around large black bags between flights. These aren't their carry-on luggage; they contain hefty airline and aircraft operations manuals, as well as maps of airports and the various landing approaches the aircraft can take.

One of the great misperceptions about pilots is that they get paid a lot for working very little. First of all, pay is usually based on seniority at an airline, so it may take many years until a pilot can fly the largest jets and achieve a higher pay scale. Some pilots are paid hardly more than schoolteachers.

It's true that pilots typically only fly seventy or eighty hours each month (the maximum is set by federal regulations and union contracts), but that only includes the time from *block to block*—pushing back from the departure gate to parking at the arrival gate. Those hours don't include checking the aircraft, figur-

The pilots' headsets are always tuned to the air traffic control radio frequencies, but the pilots also communicate with their airline's offices via private radio channels. Before takeoff, the airline's dispatcher confirms the number of passengers on board, the amount of fuel loaded, the weight of the aircraft, the takeoff speed, whether there are animals on board or in the cargo hold, and the airport's general security status.

ing fuel loads, and confirming flight plans. They also don't include the time between flights that the crew must spend away from their family and home.

All told, pilots usually spend at least 160 hours per month "at work." However, these hours are spread out. Some pilots end up working four ten-hour days a week (though they won't actually be flying for more than eight of those in each twenty-four-hour period). Other pilots are away from home for up to two weeks at a time and then may have two weeks off.

What Do the Pilots Do?

A pilot's job involves strictly following routines while constantly preparing for anything nonroutine. The two pilots on any given flight usually show up at the airport about one or two hours before takeoff and immediately start flight preparations. These include reviewing the flight plan, programming it into the autopilot system, double-checking the calculations for the fuel load, and meeting the rest of the crew (in many cases pilots at large airlines have never met each other or the flight attendants until the day of a flight).

Either the captain or the first officer performs a walkaround before each flight—often while a mechanic does a similar but separate check—looking for obvious problems or damage to the exterior of the airplane, including loose rivets, dents in the engine fan blades, or fluid dripping from unusual places. (Some fluid is okay; for example, water often drips from the air-conditioning ducts under the airplane.) It's not just a cursory check; they can be penalized if they overlook even something as "minor" as a burned-out wing lightbulb.

Back in the cockpit, the pilots also check more than 100 switches, instruments, warning lights, and circuit breakers. Can you imagine inspecting every aspect of your car (turn signals, fuses, warning lights, amount of fuel, and so on), not just once each morning but every time you wanted to drive somewhere? And even though the pilots have done this same cockpit review hundreds of times before, they don't rely on memory. One pilot reads out an item from a printed checklist, and the other pilot performs the check.

In fact, there's much more discussion between the pilots than you might expect. Besides this preflight checklist, they carefully review printed checklists while taxiing to the runway, before takeoff, after takeoff, before landing, and after landing. This somewhat obsessive routine is always the same, but that's one reason flying is so safe.

Even on a short commuter flight, pilots discuss the takeoff and flight in great detail, including calculating three important speeds:

▼ The "go/no go" velocity, called V_1. Before V_1, the pilots can stop the aircraft in an emergency; after V_1, they're committed to flying, and any emergency's more safely handled in the air.

▼ The speed at which the tail of the airplane will be rotated down, called V_r. (The tail is rotated to raise the nose and increase the angle at which the airplane is "attacking" the oncoming wind. The higher angle lets the airplane take off.)

▼ The velocity at which the aircraft will actually leave the runway, called V_2. To accommodate wind changes or other unexpected events, this is almost 30 percent faster than the aircraft actually requires to take off.

These numbers change depending on the weight of the aircraft, the amount of fuel in the tanks, the ambient temperature that day, and other factors. Then the pilots talk out the contingencies, such as who will do what if they need to abort the takeoff, and what runway they'll land on if they need to land in a hurry. This is like deciding not only the route you're going to drive to work but exactly how fast you'll enter the freeway and what you'll do if you get a flat tire during the drive.

Taking Flight

Most passengers think the captain does the flying and the first officer helps out. Actually, either one of them might be the "flying pilot" at any given time. If the two are flying multiple legs of a trip together, they might alternate flying the airplane. Sometimes both pilots work simultaneously; for instance, on takeoff, it's standard practice for both pilots to have a hand on the throttle, though only the flying pilot is really pushing. If anything happened to one pilot, the other pilot would be ready to take over instantaneously. However, while both pilots monitor the cockpit instruments and airspace, the ultimate responsibility of the flight always rests with the captain.

Pilots are typically busiest during takeoff and landing, when there's a lot going on. These are such critical times that pilots (at least those under North American regulations) are subject to a "sterile cockpit" rule: There are to be no interruptions or discussions about anything other than the operation and safety of the flight from takeoff until 10,000-feet altitude, and again from 10,000 feet down until landing.

During the flight, though, the pilots tend to be more relaxed, joking and enjoying the scenery. Pilots develop an uncanny ability to carry on a conversation while still listening to every air traffic control instruction and monitoring the cockpit instruments and radar. Of course, they can sit back partly because they're letting the autopilot do most of the work. The idea of an autopilot seems to make some passengers nervous, but computers can actually fly airplanes more smoothly than humans, making dozens of flight-path corrections each second. However, the autopilot isn't usually a completely hands-off affair; each time air traffic control tells the pilots to turn or change altitude, the flying pilot reaches over and dials the new setting into the autopilot, which then gently makes the correction.

Autopilots in many of today's jets have the ability to take off, fly, and land an airplane; some can even taxi to the gate and park (the airport also has to have special equipment for this). But pilots almost always perform takeoffs and landings themselves, as well as hand-fly the airplane up to 10,000 or 15,000 feet. After all, they became pilots because they love to fly airplanes.

Once the airplane has landed, be sure to say "thanks" to the pilots on your way out the door. Also, if you have any questions or concerns about something that happened on your flight, take a moment to ask one of the pilots about it. These folks have spent many years on their craft, and though they're often busy preparing for another flight, they really do want you to feel comfortable.

Each airline's flight operations center calculates the proper amount of fuel for an aircraft based on total weight and the distance the airplane has to travel. At takeoff, airplanes must have enough fuel to get to where they're heading, then fly to an alternate airport if necessary, and then circle in a holding pattern for a while.

There are five basic methods of navigating an airplane (or boat, or any other vehicle).

PILOTAGE: Comparing what you see on the ground with a map.

DEAD RECKONING: An unfortunate twist of the abbreviation *ded. reckoning,* from *deduced reckoning.* If you know where you started, you can deduce where you are by calculating compass direction, your air speed, wind direction, and so on.

CELESTIAL NAVIGATION: You can approximate where you are by watching the stars.

INERTIAL NAVIGATION: If you set a gyroscope spinning on a North–South axis, it will by its nature keep spinning in that direction. If you put that gyroscope on a platform that can rotate freely, you can measure how much the platform turns to always know the direction in which you're heading. Match that with sensors that measure acceleration, and you (or a computer) can calculate exactly where you are.

RADIO NAVIGATION: If you know exactly where two or more radio signals are coming from, you can accurately measure where you are in relation to those signals. There are several types of radio navigation, including VOR (Very–high–frequency Omnidirectional Range) and GPS (Global Positioning System).

These days, pilots and autopilots generally use radio and inertial navigation systems to get where they're going. Passenger airliners are always fitted with several different technologies, just in case one isn't functioning correctly.

If you've ever glanced into a cockpit (also called the *flight deck*) while boarding a flight, you probably noticed that the pilots seem to be completely surrounded by dials, knobs, buttons, and gauges. Many passengers wonder how the pilots ever make sense of it all. It turns out that it's not as complicated as it seems.

First, remember that there are *two* of every important indicator—one for each pilot. In some cases, there's even a third, which can be checked if one of the other two seem faulty. Second, many of the buttons you see (especially those little black ones on the cockpit's ceiling) are circuit breaker switches. There are hundreds of these things, and if a breaker trips (which isn't a big deal), it pops up so that it's easy to spot.

Also, there are often two or more instruments that do more or less the same thing, but in different ways. For instance, there are at least four different navigation controls, some that use gyroscopes, others that detect radio signals from the ground, a GPS unit, and so on. This kind of redundancy is one reason flying is so safe.

Pilots don't focus on any one indicator for very long; rather, they scan the instrument panel for deviations from the norm, much as you might scan the dashboard of your car to see if a warning has lit up or any dials are too high. Remember that pilots have typically flown more than 2,000 hours in other airplanes before they are even considered for a job at an airline—they've had plenty of time to get used to what looks normal in a cockpit.

Why Use Instruments

You may have also noticed how small the cockpit windows are and wondered if the pilots have a good enough view of what's going on around them. Sure, it's usually important for the pilot to see when taxiing around the airport, and the windows provide more visibility than you'd think. On clear-weather days pilots *are* responsible for paying attention and visually avoiding other aircraft (over and above the instructions from air traffic control). However, from takeoff to landing, almost every decision is based on what the pilots read on the instruments, not on what they see. In fact, the pilots could probably fly the airplane even if there were no windows at all.

The same goes for what the pilots feel. Commercial airline pilots are trained to trust the instruments more than what they feel in their bodies because it's possible to mistake sensations and become disoriented, especially when flying in a cloud or at night. For instance, the human body can sense when an airplane speeds up and slows down, but it's terrible at figuring out how fast the airplane is actually moving, especially when the speed isn't changing.

Worse, our senses cannot detect a *banked turn*. (In a banked turn, the wings are tilted and the airplane turns through the sky like a racecar on a banked racetrack.) It's not just our senses. If you hang a small weight from a string (what carpenters call a *plumb bob*), you expect that gravity will keep it pointing directly toward the earth. However, even in a steep turn, the weight actually stays pointing toward the floor of the airplane. This is why you can sit for thirty minutes oblivious to the fact that your airplane is turning in circles in a holding pattern above Chicago.

On a smaller, more nimble aircraft, you could even pour water into a cup sitting on a horizontal surface while the airplane peforms a *barrel roll* (banking and rolling all the way over, as though it were spiraling along the inside of an imaginary barrel).

In the early days of aviation, before proper instrumentation, flying in the clouds was incredibly dangerous as aircraft would turn and spin without the pilots realizing it, resulting in *death spirals*. When a pilot cannot clearly see the horizon, he or she must never make a decision based on a bodily sensation, especially if it disagrees with the cockpit instruments.

> *National Geographic* **explorer Mike Fay reports that many Africans in small villages (few of whom have ever flown) have a word for the human–made objects that they occasionally see flying overhead. They call them** *Boeings.*

The Instruments

Flight deck instruments come in all shapes, sizes, and configurations. However, whether you're in a little Cessna or a big Boeing 777, the aircraft always has four basic instruments right in front of each pilot, indicating air speed, altitude, compass heading, and attitude (that is, the artificial horizon, which offers a pictoral representation of the airplane against the outside world). In older aircraft, these are usually dials and gauges; however, most newer aircraft have "glass cockpits" in which many of the traditional instruments have been replaced with computer screens that provide the same information and more.

These are, of course, accompanied by dozens of other instruments, including engine indicators (which show engine thrust, rate of fuel consumption, speed of engine rotation, temperature of exhaust gasses, and so on), hydraulic and electrical system gauges, anti-icing controls, and radios for navigation and communication. The autopilot (plus its backup systems) usually sits between the two pilots at the top of the "dashboard," just above the landing gear controls.

On most aircraft, each pilot sits in front of a control wheel mounted on a control column. Moving the column (or "stick") forward or backward adjusts the elevators in the aircraft's tail to lower or raise the nose of the airplane. The wheel adjusts the ailerons on the wings, which—along with the rudder—help turn the aircraft. At the pilot's feet are pedals; the lower part of the pedals controls the rudder (if you press gently on the right one, the airplane turns to the right); the upper parts are wheel brakes, which of course have no use while in flight. The two sticks and wheels are connected, so that as one pilot moves a set, the other set moves, too.

There are always exceptions, however. On the jet airliners built by Airbus Industries, the control wheel is replaced by a joystick set off to the side; the pilot can move the joystick forward, backward, to the left, and to the right to control the elevators and ailerons.

Fly by Wire

There is another difference between Airbus aircraft and most other airplanes: Airbus jets are based on *fly-by-wire technology*. In a jet like the Boeing 737, the control wheel and pedals are attached to cables, pulleys, and hydraulic lines that travel from the flight deck back to the wings and tail. In fly-by-wire aircraft, however, the cockpit controls send electrical signals to computers, which in turn pass on electrical signals to mechanical actuators that adjust the flaps, ailerons, and so on.

Most newer military jets use fly-by-wire technology, as does the Boeing 777. Not only is fly-by-wire technology easier to build, maintain, and control, but it can considerably reduce the weight of an aircraft, as computers and wire weigh much less than hydraulic fluid, cables, pulleys, and the trappings of the older control systems.

Nevertheless, Airbus and Boeing still differ in their fly-by-wire philosophies. Ultimately, in fly-by-wire systems, the computer is really flying the airplane, with input from the pilots. Of course, the computer is programmed not to exceed certain constraints—maximum speed, maximum turning angle, minimum speed to avoid stall, and so on. But although an Airbus jet pilot cannot override these limitations, a Boeing 777 pilot can in an emergency.

Some industry insiders argue that Airbus trusts computers to make better decisions than pilots; others hold that Boeing is playing to characteristic American bravado. However, at the end of the day, each manufacturer has convincing arguments for why its method is better.

If you look closely at the control wheel or the control joystick in the cockpit, you'll notice one or more finger triggers or buttons. Though they look like gun triggers, the truth is much less exciting: One button lets the pilot turn the autopilot off. There is also a control for adjusting the angle of the horizontal stabilizer.

The pilots can only see about half the wing from the flight deck, and they can't see the tail at all. Some airlines are exploring the use of tiny video cameras mounted outside the aircraft to transmit images to the pilots.

Warnings

Pilots also get help from the cockpit's many electronic warning systems, which flash lights, sound sirens and bells, or "speak" messages with an electronic voice to get the pilot's attention when necessary. For example, the Traffic and Collision Avoidance System (TCAS)—standard on jet airliners—backs up the air traffic control system by monitoring all other aircraft in the vicinity during flight and constantly calculating whether any of them are on a collision course with the airplane in question. In the very rare instances when two airplanes are headed for the same airspace,

> The brakes on a jet airliner can take forty–five minutes to cool down after landing. And while jets do have parking brakes, the normal brakes cool down faster when the parking brakes are turned off, so to keep the airplane in place at the gate, the ground crew uses triangular chocks in front and back of the nose wheels.

the two TCAS systems sound a cockpit alarm and then shout at the pilots with an electronic voice to ascend or descend (the TCAS units communicate with each other, so both aircraft aren't given the same signal).

Similarly, the Ground Proximity Warning System (GPWS) constantly compares the current location of the aircraft with built-in electronic maps of the Earth's terrain. If the aircraft is headed toward the ground or a mountain, the GPWS activates an alarm that literally yells, "Pull up! Pull up!" Since 1976, when this system became standard equipment on airlines, the number of crashes due to something euphemistically called *controlled flight into terrain* has dropped radically.

Other cockpit warning systems include weather radar, wind shear detection devices, and alerts that sound off if the airplane exceeds the maximum speed, deviates from the autopilot settings, or is in danger of stalling. There are even warnings that squawk if the flaps, spoilers, stabilizers, and other control surfaces aren't in the proper position at takeoff or landing.

What Is Used?

Believe it or not, during a typical flight, pilots use about 80 or 90 percent of the knobs, dials, and switches in the cockpit (not including the circuit breakers, of course). This is one reason most pilots are rated to fly only one type of aircraft at a time. They must be able to find the right switch at the right time without hesitation, almost by reflex, and even though the Boeing 747-400 has all the same instruments as an Airbus 340, they're arranged differently. Pilots can change from one type of jet to another, but in most cases it requires intensive training.

Cockpit

WEIGHT AND BALANCE

Airplanes have to be balanced in order to fly, without too much weight on one side or the other, or too far forward or back. Engineers figure out the exact place on each airplane from which—if you had a rope big enough—you could dangle the aircraft like a giant mobile. It is then the job of the pilot and the airline to maintain that balance as much as possible when loading passengers, luggage, cargo, food, water, and fuel.

Theoretically, once an airplane is cruising along through the sky, even a single flight attendant walking to the back of the cabin could tip the aircraft's nose up very slightly. In reality, however, airlines build in such a large safety buffer to accommodate the vagaries of flying that a large jet can easily stay in balance even if 100 people got up and walked around. It's easy for the pilots (or, more likely, the autopilot) to offset imbalances by making adjustments to the power or the control surfaces on the wings and tail. However, if the airplane were really off balance—say a few tons of cargo were too far forward—the pilots would have a harder time controlling the problem.

So before each flight, the airline works out the airplane's weight and balance, taking into consideration the number of passengers in first and economy classes, the number of crew members, the amount of luggage and cargo, and so on. Instead of weighing each person before he or she flies (which was done in the early days of aviation), airlines use average weights, such as 100 pounds for a child, 150 pounds for a male flight attendant, and 25 pounds per regular bag of luggage. An adult passenger in the summer averages about 160 pounds, but in the winter weighs 5 pounds more (those heavy coats add up). Food and water add a surprising amount of weight to the airplane (water alone weighs 8.35 pounds per gallon), and where all that food is stored at the beginning of the flight is crucial.

The airline figures out how best to balance the airplane by determining how much cargo and luggage should go in which compartment under the cabin. On a very light flight with few passengers and little cargo, the airline may ask people to move forward or backward in the cabin—it's pretty rare, but it happens.

Finally, after all of the weight variables are inputted, a computer spits out the amount of fuel necessary to take off, fly to the destination, circle around for a while, and then fly to a different airport if necessary. Too much fuel can be expensive in more ways than one: It weighs more than six pounds per gallon, and the heavier the airplane, the more fuel it burns. Then the pilots calculate the proper takeoff speed based on all this information (the heavier the airplane, the faster they need to go).

On one flight out of Chicago in 1980, the pilots reported that takeoff acceleration was slower than expected and that the jet required more than the normal amount of power to take off and cruise. The flight was completed without trouble, but a later investigation found that most of the passengers on board were coin collectors traveling to a convention, and their carry-on luggage contained over a ton of coins—a bizarre circumstance not factored in by the pilots or the folks in the airline's weight and balance department.

> *A false balance is an abomination to God, but a proper balance his delight.*
>
> —*Proverbs 11:1*

If everyone on an airplane jumped into the air at the same time, would the airplane get lighter? In fact, the opposite is true. Because of a basic law of physics, every action has an equal and opposite reaction, so if you jump into the air, you actually force the airplane downward a little bit, thereby increasing its weight momentarily.

The Boeing 747–400 can carry more than its own weight. Empty, it weighs close to 200 tons, and it can carry more than 235 tons of cargo, passengers, and fuel on top of that. Total maximum weight is 875,000 pounds (about 437 tons or 400,000 kg), though it must burn off enough fuel during flight so that it weighs less than 652,000 pounds (about 325 tons or 296,000 kg) for a safe landing.

RUNWAYS

In many ways, taxiing around airport runways is more difficult for pilots than flying. Any large airport is sure to have at least two runways and over a dozen taxiways filled with airplanes at close range. In fact, it can be so confounding that pilots often familiarize themselves with detailed maps of airports before landing. Fortunately, most of the strange signs, markings, and antennae that you can see around the airport are not nearly as mysterious to pilots as they may seem to you.

For instance, runway numbers seem random, but they're not: Add 0 to the number, and you've got the runway's compass reading. On a compass, 0 degrees and 360 degrees both point north, and 180 degrees points south, so when you land on Runway 11, you're facing almost due southeast (110 degrees). The same strip of concrete approached from the opposite direction is called Runway 29. Runway 17L indicates that the airport has two parallel runways, and this is the one on the left (the other runway would be numbered both 17R and 35L).

Taxiways are named, too, and air traffic control typically instructs the pilots which runway to land on and which taxiways to use. (There's some flexibility here, however, and if a pilot misses a taxiway, he or she can usually take the next one.) Taxiway names begin with a letter, like B6 or A2, but unfortunately, each airport has its own naming conventions, so these names are somewhat arbitrary.

Runways at major air carrier airports are painted with a series of large white stripes that pilots can see

> The airport runway is the most important main-street in any town.
>
> —Norm Crabtree,
> aviation director for the state of Ohio

from a distance. First there are eight stripes along with the runway number (each digit is usually thirty feet long and ten feet wide). Five-hundred feet beyond that are six stripes—this is officially the beginning of the touchdown zone. Another 500 feet down the runway are two really thick stripes, which are what pilots aim for when landing. Finally, there are four stripes that mark 1,000 feet and 1,500 feet from the touchdown zone. Many runways also have a series of Vs at each end, ends pointed toward the center of the runway, even before the first set of stripes. In addition, there are standard lighting patterns that provide pilots with visual runway information at night.

Commercial airports also have a wide variety of antennae around the grounds. For instance, one of the most obvious is the VOR (Very-high-frequency Omni-directional Range) antenna, which looks like a white missile head coming out of a round plate. The VOR antenna beams different radio signals in each direction so that pilots can determine where they are in relation to the airport, even in low-visibility weather.

Similarly, the ILS (Instrument Landing System) antenna looks like a kids' jungle gym next to a red-and-white shack (which houses the electronics for the system). Commercial jets have special radio receivers that pick up on the ILS signal to help in the runway approach, guiding the flight path both horizontally and vertically.

To withstand the landing weight of a fully laden jumbo jet (more than 900,000 pounds), commercial airport runways are between two and four feet thick, typically with various layers of concrete and asphalt. Taxiways are often less thick, perhaps eighteen inches of concrete. It took over 2.5 million cubic yards of concrete to build Denver International airport's five 12,000-foot runways, plus taxiways.

The choice of runway is based on the prevailing wind direction because airplanes usually take off and land more or less facing into the wind.

One runway always has two numbers (one for each direction), and one number subtracted from the other always equals 18. For instance, Runway 12 and Runway 30 are the same strip of pavement because one side faces 120° (southeast) and the other faces 300° (northwest).

Tired of airplanes flying over your home? Unfortunately, you don't have much say in the matter. If you own your home, you control only about 500 or 1,000 feet of airspace above it. The law states that airplanes are allowed to fly freely above that. Individual countries do have sovereignty over the airspace above their territory, however.

The blast of air from jet engines at takeoff is so great that it would quickly erode any soil behind the runway. (Even 100 feet away, the exhaust from a 747 engine causes a 150-mph wind.) Instead of soil, some airports use precast concrete slabs seeded with hardy grass.

Runway numbering is always based on magnetic north rather than geographic (or true) north. Because the Earth's magnetic poles are about 1,000 miles (1,600 km) away from the geographic poles, true north ("up" on a map) and magnetic north (what you see on a compass) are rarely the same thing. In some places, like the state of Washington, they may differ by more than twenty degrees!

King Khalid International Airport in Riyadh, Saudi Arabia, is the world's largest airport; it covers 55,040 acres (22,016 ha). However it only serves about 8 million people each year. Chicago's O'Hare airport is about 7,000 acres (2,800 ha) and serves more than 65 million people each year.

The hotter the temperature or the higher the altitude, the thinner the air so the faster airplanes need to travel to take off (because thin air gives less of a boost). So in hot climates the runways have to be longer. The Doha runway in the Persian Gulf is 15,000 feet long. The longest runway in the world is at Edwards Air Force Base in California: 7.5 miles long.

TE D'ACCÈS A BORD/
BOARDING PASS

PAR
DESTINATION

AF 807
VOL/FLIGHT

17FEB 189

04G
SIÈGE/SEAT

CABINE

AIR FRANCE

DK NOV 80 3937-1-1

UTA

CABINE

02D
SIÈGE/SEAT

UT 771
VOL/FLIGHT

BGF
DESTINATION

09APR 5

BOARDING PASS LONDON

FIRST CLASS

NAME

SMOKING

OKING

H

THE FEAR FACTOR

Studies show that as many as half of all passengers have some qualms about flying these days. That's not surprising given the threat of terrorism, media exposés about the aviation industry, and the fact that the majority of passengers know less than you do about how airplanes work (now that you have this book). But how dangerous is flying, truly? If flying is as safe as everyone insists, why do airplanes sometimes crash? And is there anything you can do to better your chances of surviving one of those extremely rare events?

While the next few chapters look at some of the less-fun aspects of flying, they also explore the role of the flight attendant, why airplanes cause some folks so much anxiety, and why the media sometimes appear obsessed by aviation disasters.

FLIGHT STATISTICS

Human beings have a difficult time comprehending very large or very small numbers. In fact, many folks have a hard time thinking about numbers at all! But the statistics, percentages, facts, and figures involving the aviation industry are fascinating, and they help put the whole experience of commercial flight into perspective.

For instance, imagine a sports stadium filled with 45,000 people watching a game. That's not too difficult to see in the mind's eye, right? Now imagine forty of these stadiums. Most people find this harder to picture, so try pretending you're floating in a balloon over an array four stadiums wide and ten stadiums long. That's a *lot* of people. In fact, that's about the number of people who fly each day on U.S.-based airlines: about 18 million.

Who Is Flying?

About 665 *million* passengers fly on U.S.-based airlines each year—14,500 sports stadiums' worth. About 27 million passengers fly on Canadian-based airlines each year. Include the rest of the world, and the number jumps to about 1.6 *billion* passengers each year. That breaks down to about 4.25 million people (approximately the entire population of Norway) getting on airplanes every day of the year.

New Scientist magazine figured that given the total number of people flying each day and the average distance flown per flight (around 1,100 miles, or 1,750 km), there are about 366,144 people in the air at any given time. While that's the equivalent to the population of a medium-sized city, it's only about .0061 percent of the world population. Of course, in reality the number of people fluctuates greatly depending on the time of day, day of the week, and week of the year.

> *Airplane travel is nature's way of making you look like your passport photo.*
>
> —*Former vice president Albert Gore*

According to the U.S. National Transportation Safety Board (NTSB), in the year 2000 U.S.-based commercial airlines alone flew a total of 11,022,759 flights, covering 7,148,928,000 miles in 17,474,405 flight hours. That's equivalent to 13,000 round-trip voyages to the Moon.

How Safe Is Flying?

Thinking about extremely small figures can be just as mind-numbing as trying to comprehend the very large ones above. For example, one way to reckon airline safety is by the percentage of airplane flights that crash with at least one fatality. What if air travel were 99.99 percent safe? That would result in three fatal air crashes every day of the year. In fact, air travel is approximately 99.9999996 percent safe. That means only about .0000004 percent of airplanes crash.

But that number is simply too small to be meaningful for most people. Instead, they just think, "Well, it *seems* like I hear about a lot of disasters."

Let's look at some real safety numbers:

▼ More people die in car crashes in North America in six months than have died in all the airplane accidents worldwide in the last 100 years.

▼ If air travel were as safe as driving in a car, a jet aircraft carrying 120 people would crash without survivors every day of the year.

▼ Air Canada has only had 3 fatal accidents since 1970, and the last was in 1983.

▼ Of the approximately 2.5 million Americans who died in 1998, more than 700,000 died of heart disease, some 500,000 died from cancer, at least 50,000 died from medical mistakes in hospitals, and more than 20,000 died in car crashes. But not a single passenger died from U.S.-based airliners crashing. Even in 1994, a year with a higher-than-average number of disasters, only 239 people died.

▼ The U.S. Bureau of Travel Statistics reports that in 1995 (the most current information available) Americans took approximately 505 million automobile trips of 100 miles or more, and about 22,000 car passengers died. That same year, U.S. air carriers flew about 8.1 million flights, and there were two crashes in which 166 people died. If the average car had 2 people and the average flight had 150 people, there were 22 fatalities per million automobile trips and only .14 fatalities per million air trips—air travel was 157 times safer than driving.

▼ Because people generally drive much more than they fly, let's look at the relative safety of cars and airplanes based on the distance they travel rather than the number of trips. The U.S. National Safety Council calculates that between 1993 and 1999, passengers were thirty-seven times more likely to die in a car crash than on a commercial flight. Using more conservative crash data, the U.S. Bureau of Transportation Statistics calculated the number of fatalities per 100 million miles of long-distance travel: 9.3 for cars, 5 for trains, and 1.22 for commercial airlines. Here, flying is almost eight times safer than driving, and almost twice as safe as taking the train.

According to a study by Arnold Barnett and Alexander Wang of the Massachusetts Institute of Technology, the odds of dying in an airplane crash vary slightly depending on whether you're on an international or domestic flight, and whether the airline is from an industrial or developing nation. For domestic flights on an industrial nation's airline, the odds of dying are about one in 8 million (you have a better chance at winning many state lotteries). Small commuter airplanes in the United States fare slightly worse: The odds are about one in 2 million.

For international flights, the odds of a fatality drop to one in 5 million—curiously, this figure is about the same whether it's an industrial or developing nation's airline. Finally, domestic flights on developing nations' jet airlines have the highest fatality odds of all: one in 500,000. That sounds bad, but one in 500,000 is like saying "one day out of 1,300 years."

According to the Air Transportation Association, 26 percent of Americans took at least one airplane flight in 1978. By 1997, the numbers had swelled to 48 percent. The U.S. Bureau of Travel Statistics reports that one out of six adults in the United States has never flown on a commercial airline.

The odds of your flight crashing are always the same, no matter how often you fly. However, the more frequently you fly, the higher the chance you will someday crash (just like the more lottery tickets you buy, the more likely you are to win). Fortunately for frequent flyers, the difference is incredibly small. If 1,000 people flew every day for thirty years, only one of them would likely crash.

Vast Quantities

The infrastructure necessary to maintain millions of flights each week is staggering. For instance, Delta Airlines (the third largest airline in the United States) sells approximately 316,000 airline tickets each day for its 2,660 daily flights (that's 3 tickets every second and an airplane departure every thirty-two seconds around the clock). Each day, Delta flights burn about 7.5 million gallons of jet fuel and carry about 2,333 tons of mail. To keep the passengers happy, flight attendants on this airline alone serve 164,400 meals or snacks, 461,000 soft drinks, and 225,500 cups of coffee (give or take a few).

So the next time you're on a flight, munching happily on your pretzels or

According to the U.S. National Safety Council, more Americans die each year by drowning in their bathtubs, falling from ladders, or freezing to death than by flying on commercial airlines.

nuts, consider the numbers, the odds, and the percentages . . . and as your mind begins to boggle, sit back and smile, knowing that you're not alone and you're very safe.

WHY AIRPLANES SOMETIMES CRASH

There is something about airplane crashes—something gruesomely compelling—that makes people take notice. Perhaps airplane crashes capture our attention because so many people die at the same time. Even a crash that kills only 10 or 20 people becomes national or international news. Of course, more than 2,000 people die each day from heart disease in the United States alone, but they're spread out geographically so this doesn't have the same impact.

Airline crashes are extremely rare (see the preceding chapter, "Flight Statistics"), and fatal crashes are even rarer. Even so, studies show that most air travel passengers believe that in 75 percent of airline accidents some or all the passengers die. After all, they reason, how could anyone survive an airplane crash? However, in 86 percent of commercial airline accidents, nobody dies at all. Even in crashes where there is a loss of life, over half the passengers survive on average.

Nevertheless, as rare as airplane crashes are, there's no denying that they do happen and that they are scary. With this in mind, let's look at why airplanes can crash and what has been done to make flying safer.

Determining the Cause

When discussing an airline disaster, people like to point to one or two major problems and say, "That's why the airplane crashed." But airplanes almost never crash because of one or two problems. For example, ever since 1982, when an Air

Captain Moody made this announcement after his British Airways 747 flew through the volcanic ash shot into the sky by the 1982 eruption of Mount Galunggung in Indonesia. The 747 lost power in all four engines but glided long enough to exit the ash cloud and get three engines working again. The airplane's windshield was so sandblasted by ash that the landing had to be made almost entirely by instruments, and the airplane had to be towed to the gate because the pilots couldn't see enough to taxi around the airport.

There are many ways to make airplanes safer, but there is also a point of diminishing returns. Each safety feature costs money, which makes the price of flying higher, which means more people would drive instead of fly, which would lead to more injuries and fatalities (because driving is significantly more dangerous than flying).

Florida jet crashed just after takeoff from National Airport in Washington, D.C., the public has remembered "there was ice and snow on the wings." But in fact, ice and snow don't necessarily make an airplane crash, and if it hadn't been for other circumstances this one certainly could have flown given those conditions.

The true story is always more complicated, and it usually involves at least five or six factors. Yes, ice played a part in the Air Florida crash, but few people remember the other details—for example, the pilots relied on a particular engine pressure gauge, even though there was plenty of evidence to suggest that the reading was incorrect. If any one factor of many had been different—if only there were no snowstorm, if only the airplane had been deiced more recently, if only a sensor hadn't malfunctioned, if only the pilots had given the airplane more thrust at takeoff, and so on—the disaster would have been averted.

One factor that almost always appears in airline accident reports is human error—whether by the flight crew, air traffic control, mechanics, or airport security. Paradoxically, the most important reason flying is so safe—the reliance on the extraordinary training and skill of the people involved—is also one of aviation's prime weaknesses. Airplanes crash for all sorts of reasons, from mechanical failures to acts of terror, from miscommunications to misunderstandings, but it is almost always an extremely rare combination of factors that leads to a disaster.

It's understandable that people who have plans to fly get nervous after seeing a news story about a crash; after all, it's difficult not to compare your flight with the one that crashed. However, air disasters these days rarely have anything to do with the particular kind of aircraft, the time of day the crash occurred, or even the weather. Changing your reservations makes little sense since the chances of the same five or six incredibly improbable events happening at the same time are so slim.

> Attempting to emergency-land an aircraft in the water is called *ditching*.

> The airline industry has come a long way since the first decade of commercial flight, when thirty-one of the first forty airmail pilots were killed in crashes.

Making Flying Safer

The aviation industry has developed two basic methods for improving flying safety over the years. First, every important system on an airplane has at least one backup system and often three or more redundant backups. The aviation industry simply assumes that there will be occasional human or mechanical errors, and takes this into account when designing airplanes. For instance:

▼ There are two pilots when one could do the job in a pinch.

▼ There are typically four or five separate navigational devices, including three or four different radio systems.

▼ If one engine of a twin-engine airplane quits (*flames out*), even on takeoff, the other engine is powerful enough to fly the airplane by itself.

▼ On airplanes that rely on hydraulic power to move the control surfaces on the wings and tail, there are usually two or even four separate hydraulic systems (pumps, fluid lines, and so on). If one goes out, another can take its place in an instant.

▼ Every important instrument or indicator in the cockpit has an identical twin (or even triplet). That's like having two or three speed dials in your car, just in case one fails.

Second, the aviation industry runs on a "never again" system, in which each problem—from a minor rattle to a major crash—is reported, investigated, and if necessary, fixed on all other relevant aircraft so that it won't occur again. Similarly, because most airline disasters involve some level of human error, pilots, controllers, mechanics, and cabin crews may anonymously report potentially dangerous behavior to NASA's Aviation Safety Reporting System so that even errors that haven't (yet) caused an accident or reportable incident may still be studied and contribute to improved safety.

This system of constant review and fleet-wide maintenance has meant that the kinds of airline disasters that happened twenty, ten, or even five years ago are much less likely to occur today. In the early 1970s an explosion inside a jet engine released a fan blade which pierced both the engine cowling and fuselage and killed one passenger. The aircraft landed safely, but engines have been made safer ever since; today, the engines on the Boeing 777 are surrounded by three inches of Kevlar to contain even a massive engine failure.

After a crash of a Boeing 767 in 1991, investigators were mystified as to why one engine's thrust reversers kicked in during a flight. After all, the 767 was (and is) considered one of the safest types of aircraft, and there was simply no reason why this might have happened. The result: Boeing finally decided to redesign the thrust reverser's electrical system and retrofitted nearly 2,000 aircraft, just in case this was the cause of the disaster.

One curious side effect of the "never again" system is that it can be more difficult to identify clear causes for some of the crashes that occur these days. Thirty years ago, investigators could relatively quickly point to problems such as metal fatigue or flying into wake turbulence (the intense vortices that follow large jets). Since then, systems have been put in place to avoid those problems. Flying has been made so much safer that airplanes only crash under extremely odd circumstances.

Not knowing is, of course, more frightening than knowing why something happened. That's one reason the mysterious midair explosions of TWA 800 in 1996 and SwissAir 111 in 1998 are so scary. But Boeing, Airbus, and other manufacturers continue to redesign aircraft to counter even the few "might have beens" that could have caused these disasters.

If Problems Arise

Most airline pilots will fly their entire careers without having as much as a "close call," and it's a very rare pilot indeed who will be involved in an accident. But on those rare occasions when a series of improbable things go wrong and an accident occurs, it's important to remember three things: Pilots are extensively trained to handle emergencies; airplanes are designed to withstand significant malfunctions; and a whole lot can go wrong without anyone getting killed.

For example, commercial airplanes are designed to land even without land-

Those "black boxes" that contain cockpit voice recordings and flight data are designed to survive intense impacts, fire, and even being immersed in saltwater at a pressure equivalent to 20,000 feet below sea level for thirty days. Why don't they just make the whole airplane out of the same material? Because it would be so heavy that it would never get off the ground, of course.

Many passengers became nervous about flying on the MD-80 aircraft after Alaska Airlines Flight 261 crashed in 2000. However, the statistics are clear: The MD-80 is the safest jet aircraft in history, with only eight fatal crashes out of 20 million flights. According to AirDisaster.com, the next safest aircraft are: Boeing 767, 757, 737, and the Airbus A320.

ing gear, by skidding along the runway. In fact, no one in recent history has been seriously hurt in a landing of this sort. One of the most astonishing displays of how robust commercial airplanes are occurred in 1988, when a stress fracture on an Aloha Airlines flight caused one-third of the top of the fuselage to rip off the airplane while it was in flight. Sadly, a flight attendant was pulled out of the airplane and killed, but the pilots safely landed the aircraft—even with a giant hole in it—saving the lives of all the passengers.

Ironically, flying at cruising altitude is typically the safest time for something to go wrong because there is plenty of time and space to recover. A severe downdraft or wind shear is scary at cruising altitude, but not life-threatening if you have a seatbelt on. On the other hand, in the case of an on-board fire, it's much better to be near the ground and preferably near an airport with fire trucks.

What You Can Do

Even though there are only about thirty emergency evacuations of aircraft each year in the United States (out of more than 10 million flights), it's worth knowing what to expect and what you should do, just in case. Most people think it's unlikely that an airplane could be evacuated quickly—after all, consider how long it takes for people to exit the airplane normally. But airline manufacturers must demonstrate that a full aircraft can be evacuated within ninety seconds, using only half the available exits, and in the dark. (When the Boeing 777 was being tested, one volunteer out of 420 refused to jump down the evacuation slide during the allotted time, so the FAA rated the aircraft for only 419 passengers.)

Here are some other things you should keep in mind in case of an emergency:

> One of the main reasons airlines turn off the main cabin lights during nighttime takeoffs and landings is to prepare the passengers' eyesight for dim light in case of an emergency that requires evacuation in the dark.

▼ If the oxygen masks pop out, don't hesitate to put one on. Flight attendants report that many passengers just stare at the masks until they're told to use them or until they pass out. (At cruise altitudes, you probably have about fifteen or twenty seconds before you lose consciousness.) Remember that you must tug on the oxygen tube in order to release a pin; otherwise, the oxygen won't flow at all. You probably won't feel the oxygen or see the oxygen bag inflate at first because it's supposed to inflate when you breathe out.

▼ If the aircraft really has lost its air pressure (*rapid decompression*), the pilot will quickly descend to a safe altitude. Don't panic; airplanes can fly just fine in this situation.

▼ If you know there is going to be a sudden deceleration (what most people would call a crash landing), watch out for the heavy stuff in the bins above you as it will almost certainly fall out. Get into the emergency brace position: If you have the room, lean over and grab your legs or ankles. Otherwise, cross your arms on the chair back of the seat in front of you and rest your head on your arms.

▼ Whenever possible, watch and listen to the flight attendants. They are extensively trained. However, if you can't hear or see one, use your best judgment and be prepared to get out on your own. (On the other hand, don't overreact; passengers have been known to open exits and jump out while the airplane was still on the taxiway because of engine smoke or flames, an uncommon but non-life-threatening event.)

▼ Believe it or not, a large percentage of people refuse to leave their seats after an emergency landing. There may only be a few minutes to get out of the airplane safely, so if you see people just sitting frozen, get them to move.

▼ If the cabin is filling with smoke, bend low but don't drop to your hands and knees. This way, you'll still be able to move quickly. Also, cover your nose and mouth with a cloth (wet if possible), such as a T-shirt or napkin.

▼ Forget your carry-on bags. Anything you try to take with you may mean the difference between life and death—either for you or for someone else behind you. Getting passengers to leave their bags is one of the biggest challenges flight attendants face during an evacuation.

▼ People tend to try to return to the front-most door where they entered the airplane rather than use the exits over the wings or at the back of the aircraft. This is a recipe for disaster; use whatever exit is closest to you and is open.

▼ Don't push anybody, and don't let anyone push you. If one person falls, it may impede everyone's evacuation. Similarly, don't crowd the exit doors—remember that they must open inward before they swing out.

▼ Before going down an escape slide, remove your shoes; they might catch on the slide (damaging you, other passengers, or the inflatable slide itself). Hold on to them if you can, though, as there may be broken glass on the ground.

▼ Many injuries during evacuations come from people running into each other or falling off the end of the slide, so once you're out of the airplane, move away as quickly as possible.

Ultimately, the most important rule is: Don't Panic. Given the extraordinary resources that have gone into making flying—and even crashing—as safe as possible, chances are that you will be okay.

A Sigh of Relief

If flying is getting safer, why do some news stories insist that the number of fatalities worldwide in the 1990s actually increased over those in the 1980s? Because that's only half the story. It's true that during the 1980s about 1,060 people died each year (almost 90 percent of that number were on non-U.S. airlines) from crashes, and that in the 1990s, the number rose by about 12.5 percent. However, airlines flew over *30 percent* more passengers and flights in the 1990s, so the average risk to passengers actually decreased significantly.

However, even though flying is one of the safest forms of transportation (other than perhaps the elevator), there are risks involved. Everybody on an airplane—even the pilots—breathes a quiet sigh of relief when the wheels touch down safely on the runway. It's a good time to be grateful to the pilots, the attendants, and the aviation community that is so determined to transport you safely and efficiently.

> *It's always a good idea to keep the pointy end going forward as much as possible . . . A "good" landing is one from which you can walk away. A "great" landing is one after which they can use the plane again.*
>
> *—From an anonymous list of flying "rules" for pilots*

BE PREPARED: WHAT YOU CAN DO TO SURVIVE AN EMERGENCY

The chances that you will ever be in an airplane accident are miniscule, no matter how often you fly. Nevertheless, there are things you can do to be prepared. Most crashes are survivable, and evidence shows that the people who typically survive are those who are ready for the worst. Here are a few ideas you might keep in mind when preparing for a flight.

▼ Wear comfortable clothing that covers you well, as opposed to short pants or skirts. Neckties can restrict breathing, hairspray is flammable, and pantyhose and other synthetic clothing may melt to the skin if there is a fire or from the friction from sliding down an emergency slide.

▼ Even in a normal flight, the air pressure causes our feet and ankles to swell, so wear loose-fitting pants and shoes. However, shoes should have fasteners because you're likely to lose sandals or high heels in a crash landing.

▼ If you take medications, keep them in your pocket rather than in a handbag or carry-on, which will be difficult or impossible to access in the event of an emergency.

▼ Find the closest exits in front of you and behind you, and count the number of seat rows to them. If smoke fills the cabin, it will be nearly impossible to see an exit sign and you'll have to find an exit by memory. Many aircraft are now fitted with emergency floor lighting that can also help direct you to the exits.

▼ Keep one of those airline blankets nearby; they're flame retardant and are good to duck under in case of fire.

▼ If possible, infants should be fastened into a car seat that can be buckled into the airplane chair. It you can't afford a separate seat (even at infant rates), then at least use a restraining system, which attaches to your seatbelt, in case of severe turbulence.

▼ Your seatbelt should be snug across your lap. A loose seatbelt can actually cause internal injuries in an accident.

▼ Don't worry about where you're sitting; no one area on an airplane is any safer than any other.

It's also important to listen to the preflight safety message, even if you've heard it before. If you think it's silly for the flight attendants to explain things like how to open a seatbelt, think again: A surprisingly large percentage of people freeze up and can't get out of their seatbelts in an emergency. Similarly, life vests can be complicated; when watching the flight attendant put one on, visualize putting one on yourself. (After all, about 70 percent of all airports are near the water.)

Don't be embarassed to look over the emergency safety card, too, especially if you're in an emergency row—people's lives (including your own) depend on you knowing this material.

THE MEDIA'S FASCINATION WITH AIRLINE DISASTERS

If you ask the average person-on-the-street what he or she knows about airplanes, you will probably hear about some well-known crashes, but almost nothing about how airplanes work the other 99.9999 percent of the time. This isn't surprising given the fact that most people get their information from television, radio, and newspapers. Since the dawn of aviation, the media have found that airplane disasters attract attention like few other stories.

On the one hand, the intense media scrutiny actually makes the airline industry safer by putting pressure on the government and the airlines. But on the other hand, the media's tendency toward frightening pictures and sensationalist headlines has made many people nervous about flying.

For example, the media knows you'll read about the 292 people who died in U.S.-based airline disasters in 1994. It's simply human nature to be drawn to this kind of story, even though it's frightening to think, "That could have been me." However, who would buy a newspaper with the true headline, "*Nobody* died in U.S.-airline crashes in 2002"? Sadly, reassuring statistics are rarely considered news.

Selling the Story

Of course, with all due respect to the commercial media, it's important to remember that their primary goal isn't to inform you; their goal is to sell advertising. And the most effective method of selling advertising is to hold your attention with a compelling, scary story.

Journalists even use the term *stories* to talk about the news. They know that their job is to gather the facts as best they can and then spin them into a story worthy of telling around a campfire (or the water cooler). Unfortunately, sometimes the story overwhelms the facts. For example, in 1994 *USA Today* printed a front-page article that stated, "Steer clear of commuter planes with fewer than 30 seats and 'don't even consider flying them at night or in bad weather' warns a consumer group." However, less clear was that the consumer group included Alaskan bush flights, helicopters, and air taxis in their research. If you take those out, the statistics are clear: Commuter airplanes are just about as safe as larger aircraft. And, of course, even those riskier forms of flying are still safer than most other forms of transportation. (To its credit, the newspaper did publish a small follow-up article about this several days later, but printed it on page 12.)

After the Accident

As you might expect, the vast majority of aviation news coverage occurs immediately after a plane crash. As Barry Glassner points out in his book *The Culture of Fear*, after the 1996 crash of ValueJet Flight 592, some major newspapers and television networks—including the *New York Times*, CBS, and NBC—ran about fifty news stories *each* in just two weeks.

Unfortunately, in the first few days after an accident, much of the information in the media is wrong because it is based on speculation and hearsay. In most instances, it's simply impossible for anyone to know all the factors that caused a crash within a week (or even a month) of the event. However, news is perishable and the media can't wait to get the facts, so instead they use the "shotgun" method, reporting everything that *might* have gone wrong.

Then, once the real facts do begin to appear, they're hardly reported because the accident is "yesterday's news." When was the last time you saw a headline read, "We were wrong; this issue isn't actually something you need to worry about"?

Ultimately, although there are certainly reputable aviation journalists who know enough to avoid spreading untruths, it's generally a good idea to be somewhat skeptical when reading, listening, or viewing reports about the aviation industry.

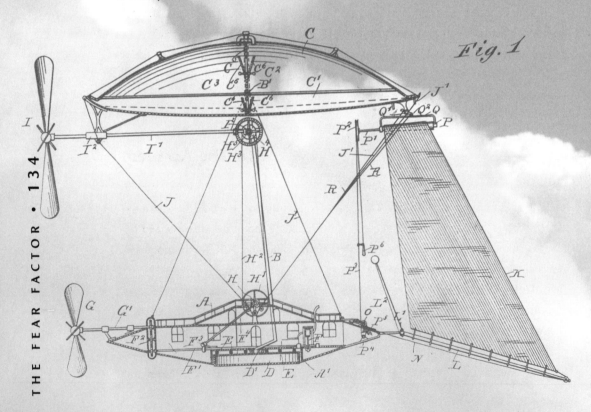

Fig. 1

LESS STRESS, MORE FUN

There's something about flying that can make some folks act in crazy ways, screaming at the check-in counter staff, or even attacking flight attendants. In fact, according to the flight attendants union, each year there are several thousand instances of "air rage," including several hundred cases of physical abuse. Alcohol (which loosens inhibitions) and caffeine (which raises the blood pressure) often contribute to the problem, but the underlying condition that breeds this rage is likely the overwhelming feeling of not being in control.

Perhaps the feeling starts in the car, on the way to the airport, as the traffic slows to a crawl and you begin to wonder if you'll arrive in time for your flight. Perhaps you feel a tightening in your stomach while waiting in the surprisingly long check-in line, or the security line, or the boarding line—speculating about everything from turbulence to terrorists. Perhaps your flight has been delayed or canceled, and you miss your connection or business meeting. Perhaps your flight is so full that you and your spouse can't sit next to each other, or you're stuck in a middle seat at the back of the airplane across from the toilet.

True, when you're flying you're definitely not in control. Worse, the experience of flying is nowhere near as pleasant as it used to be, or as it appears to be in television ads. In this age of overbooked flights and tightened security—when every step from parking your car to finding your luggage at the end of the flight can be a struggle—it's

> In the space age, man will be able to go around the world in two hours—one hour for flying and one hour to get to the airport.
>
> —Neil McElroy,
> former U.S. secretary of defense

> I once saw a flight attendant charging down the aisle looking so distressed I was sure we were all goners, but it turned out that somebody was trying to pay for a beer with a $50 bill.
> —Layne Ridley, WHITE KNUCKLES

> You define a good flight by negatives: you didn't get hijacked, you didn't crash, you didn't throw up, you weren't late, you weren't nauseated by the food. So you're grateful.
> —Paul Theroux, Novelist and travel writer

almost understandable that people occasionally snap.

Sometimes people become belligerent when they are told that they cannot use their cell phones during the flight, or when a flight attendant refuses to serve them alcohol (flight attendants cannot legally give alcohol to someone who is already obviously drunk). Passengers have slapped and even punched crew members; on one occasion, a passenger ended up breaking the neck of a gate agent. Fortunately, these instances are rare, but they are proof that air rage has become a reality.

Here are a few ways to reduce your stress (and that of those around you) with a few precautions:

▼ Get to the airport far earlier than you need to. This way, you can breathe easy through bad traffic or long lines at the airport, and you can always read a book or explore the airport if you have extra time.

▼ Remember that some airlines will cancel your reservation if you don't check in within ten or twenty minutes of the flight.

▼ Be as pleasant as you can to the airline staff, especially if you want them to be pleasant to you.

▼ Never physically interfere with a flight attendant; in the United States, it's a federal crime, punishable by up to twenty years in prison and a $25,000 fine.

▼ Avoid alcohol before or during the flight.

▼ If you want to chat with the stranger next to you, be sensitive that he or she might not want to talk (grunting or offering monosyllabic answers to your questions is a good indicator). Or if your seatmate wants to talk and you don't, just be honest and say, "I'm sorry, but I rarely get any quiet time, and I'm not much in the mood for talking." (Or lie and say you work for a tax collection service like the IRS; that usually works.)

If God had really intended men to fly, He'd make it easier to get to the airport.
—Humorist George Winters

(Courtesy of Airbus Industrie)

> *That is the trouble with flying: We always have to return to airports. Think of how much fun flying would be if we didn't have to return to airports.*
> —Henry Mintzberg, WHY I HATE FLYING

Ever since 1912, when Calbraith Perry Rogers was killed after a seagull flew into his airplane's motor, aviators have been keenly aware that birds and airplanes in flight don't mix. Today, as some bird populations such as the non-migratory Canada geese are on the rise, and there are more airplanes flying than ever, trying to keep the two apart is getting harder. The "bird strike" problem is greatest when airplanes are taking off and landing, so airports are using a wide variety of techniques to keep birds away, including nonlethal chemical repellents, audiotapes simulating birds in distress, trained falcons, "hot foot" (a sticky chemical that irritates birds' feet), "Nixalite" (a roll of spikes that stops birds from landing), floating plastic balls that cover ponds, and even border collies trained to herd birds. On occasion, airports simply send someone out to shoot the birds.

RETAIN THIS FOR RES

Please Note: Your seat has
please return
inconveniences
on this flight

FIRST CLASS

ECONOMY

1 — 7

ECONOMY
No Smoking

DC10 8–22
DC 8 8–16

ECONOMY
• 1 3 9

23 – 34

BEHIND THE SCENES AT THE AIRLINE

The only aspect of aviation more amazing than the fact that jumbo jets can actually get off the ground is the intricate and interwoven system of logistics that makes it possible for the commercial airline system to move millions of people around the globe each day. Most passengers take for granted that airplanes will depart more or less on time and get them to their destination securely and comfortably— more or less. However, passengers see only a small handful of the tens of thousands of people who work at each major airport and airline—the crew schedulers, the meteorologists, the weight and balance staff, the caterers, the fuel crew, and more.

In the next several chapters, we'll take a quick look behind the scenes, exploring some of the systems that are working twenty-four hours a day to help fly you from place to place.

SCHEDULED DEPARTURES

Perhaps it's of little comfort, but the next time your airplane lands thirty minutes late, remember the seventeenth-century clipper ships. No one ever expected them to deliver their loads of passengers and cargo on schedule; in fact, everyone rejoiced if a ship arrived in the right week or month—or even arrived at all. The point is that it's relatively easy to keep airplanes flying, but it's extremely difficult to keep them flying on schedule.

One of the biggest challenges to a firm schedule is the weather. No airline will fly its aircraft (or passengers) in a thunderstorm or hurricane, so teams of meterologists work around the clock to spot and predict wind conditions, precipitation, and anything else that could cause a delay around the globe. A storm in the Arctic could seriously hamper flights between New York and Hong Kong that fly near the North Pole. Warmer-than-average ocean currents could shift the position of high-altitude jet streams and add an hour to a cross-country flight.

Worst of all, a thunderstorm hovering over a major hub could cause disruptions around the world. Chicago's O'Hare airport is the busiest airport in the world, with over 900,000 flights departing each year (Atlanta's Hartsfield International is a close second); if it closes for six hours, flight schedules can be affected globally. After all, a jet leaving Chicago may be needed in Washington, D.C., so that it can take a flight to Los Angeles, and its captain can fly a different jet to Buenos Aires. Most airlines have a rule: Always inconvenience the fewest number of passengers. So if that flight to Los Angeles has 220 passengers, many of whom are making connecting flights to Australia and Asia, and there is another airplane flying from Washington, D.C., to Denver with only 50 people on it, the airline may cancel the Denver flight and use the airplane to fly to Los Angeles instead. That's why you may later hear an announcement that your flight is delayed due to "weather," even though it's a beautiful day outside.

> *When the weight of the paperwork equals the weight of the airplane, you're ready to take off.*
> —Pilot's saying

The same thing happens on a smaller scale when an aircraft has mechanical difficulties or if a passenger has a medical emergency and the aircraft has to reroute. Sometimes a long delay will push a landing time past an airport's night curfew, and the flight has to be rerouted or canceled. Airlines can't afford to keep extra $50-million airplanes around to fill in the gaps created by an unexpected delay, so even seemingly minor disruptions can cause ripples throughout the system.

To avoid differences in time zones, everyone in the airline industry uses Coordinated Universal Time (UTC), or "Zulu" time (so called because "Zulu" designates the letter *z*, which represents zero). UTC used to be called Greenwich Mean Time (GMT) because it is based on the time in Greenwich, England—also the location of the prime meridian (zero degrees longitude).

Another, perhaps more infuriating reason for delays is that airlines regularly schedule more aircraft departures than some airports can actually safely accommodate. In many cases, airplanes leave the gate on time only to stand in a long line of other airplanes waiting for a runway because *on-time departure* technically means a plane leaving the gate on time, not necessarily taking off when it's supposed to.

Of course, it's always maddening to hear that your flight has been canceled, especially if the reason seems mysterious. The gate agents may announce a delay or cancellation due to mechanical problems (because that's what the airline told them), but this doesn't necessarily mean the problem was on that particular aircraft. There's little doubt that some gate agents (or their superiors) lie to passengers to keep complaints down. After all, no passenger wants to hear, "The airline has decided it's more economical to cancel your flight than to inconvenience these other people." More often than not, however, everyone is telling the truth—or at least, as much of the truth as they know.

To keep things flowing smoothly, every two hours in the United States, representatives from the major airlines and the U.S. Federal Aviation Administration (FAA) have a conference telephone call to discuss how things are going and what the airlines should expect in the next few hours: weather concerns, delays, overscheduling, and so on.

People Movers

Another giant challenge to maintaining an on-time schedule is the logistical nightmare of having the right crew on the right flights at the right time. Step into the central operations room of any large airline, and you'll find almost 100 people whose job it is to track the thousands of flight and ground crew employees. A rerouted flight may bump a pilot up against her maximum legal flight-hour limits, making it impossible for her to fly another leg of a trip. A flight attendant who calls in sick needs to be replaced in order for the flight to take off. A mechanical difficulty could strand pilots and attendants for hours in one city when they're needed on flights elsewhere.

Flight crews (pilots and flight attendants) typically don't remain on the same airplane, or even remain together as a team, for more than one or two legs of a flight. Instead, they are individually routed from airport to airport, either working on a flight or flying as a passenger, often called *jump-seating* or *dead-heading*. (*Jump-seating* also describes flying on your own or another airline for free or next-to-free, one of the perks of working in this industry. *Dead-heading* also describes flying an airplane from one city to another with no one but a few crew members aboard in order to pick up passengers or have mechanical repairs, sometimes called *ferrying*.)

Flight crew supervisors have to track a large number of factors, like the number of hours each person has worked in a day or a month, the kind of aircraft each pilot is rated to fly (you can't put a Boeing 747 pilot in an Airbus 319), and where each person lives in relation to his or her flight. For instance, many pilots live in a different city than their *domicile* (the city from which their flights typically originate), so a pilot might have to take a ninety-minute flight just to show up for work in the morning.

Similarly, other supervisors are working around the clock tracking ground crew members, ensuring that airline representatives show up at the proper gate an hour before each flight, that agents are ready to help people make tight connections, and that the staff is ready to help guide an arriving aircraft in, unload baggage, fill the plane with fuel, and so on.

> The shortest flight in the world is British Airways' twice-daily Flight 872 between Westray and Papa Westray, Scotland, which takes just two minutes.

> The world's longest flight is currently United Airlines' nonstop Flight 821 between New York and Hong Kong (via the North Pole), which spans 8,439 miles in fifteen hours, forty minutes.

> It's no coincidence that in no known language does the phrase "As pretty as an airport" appear.
>
> —Douglas Adams,
> THE LONG DARK TEA-TIME OF THE SOUL

AIRPLANE FOOD

The next time you look down and grimace at whatever meal a flight attendant has placed before you, take a moment and consider your food's astonishing history. While a few airlines still run their own kitchens, most airlines contract out to one of two companies—Dobbs (which is part of the Gate Gourmet conglomerate) or LSG Sky Chefs—each of which runs hundreds of kitchens around the globe. These "kitchens" are actually enormous manufacturing plants, with hundreds of workers on assembly lines putting out thousands of trays of food each day. The larger kitchens can produce more than 8 million meals each year.

In fact, in a single year just one of these large catering kitchens reported using some 2.7 million eggs, 22 tons of smoked salmon, 75 tons of carrots, 274,000 packets of strawberry jam, and 183,000 heads of lettuce. Chefs combine their raw materials into entrées which are individually wrapped, quick-frozen at temperatures below -238°F (-150°C), and then placed in enormous multistory refrigerated warehouses. Each day, the proper number of meals, called *pop-outs*, can then be pulled, thawed, and loaded into containers along with trays, glasses, flatware, napkins, salads, rolls, desserts, and whatever else the airline has paid for. Each meal must look as identical as possible, as passengers tend to compare their meals to their neighbors'.

Getting the right meals to the right flight at the right time is a feat that requires near-military precision and is made even trickier by the increasing number of special meals that passengers order. Today, airlines offer more meal choices than ever: vegetarian (dairy or nondairy), low-fat, low-cholesterol, low-salt, gluten-free, diabetic, hot or cold seafood, fruit plate, Asian, children's, Kosher, Hindu, Muslim, and more. Some airlines have special McDonald's meals for kids, others offer warm chocolate chip cookies; American Airlines offers Weight Watchers' meals on some flights, and Alaska Airlines added Alaskan wild berry jams and reindeer sausages to some breakfasts. Almost all special meals must be ordered twenty-four hours in advance.

> The more I fly, the more I'm convinced that the true wonder of modern aviation is the transformation of tasteless particles into something known as airplane food.
>
> —Bob Blumer, THE SURREAL GOURMET

Catering companies must be extremely careful about not only security (after all, these items will be loaded onto an airplane) but also food safety—the meals must be kept cool and be transferred onto the airplane as quickly as possible. Those in-flight food trolleys are often loaded with dry ice to keep their contents cool throughout the flight.

One kitchen may make meals for a number of different airlines, and each airline has its own menus, dishes, flatware, and tray style. A single Boeing 747 typically requires the catering company to load more than 40,000 individual items for an international flight. That means each kitchen must juggle hundreds of thousands of pieces of cutlery, glasses, trays, and other reusable items each day.

It's hard to imagine these economies of scale. U.S.-based airlines spent over $3.4 billion on in-flight service in 2000. Southwest Airlines—perhaps the king of the "no frills" airlines—spent almost $15 million serving over 95 million bags of peanuts and drinks. Even so, that translates to less than twenty-five cents per passenger; according to *USA Today*, Delta Airlines spent about $3 per passenger on food in 1999, United Airlines spent about $4.75, and American Airlines spent over $6 for each of its tens of millions of passengers.

If an airline can save a penny by altering its menu, it can reduce its yearly expenses by hundreds of thousands of dollars. One airline reportedly saved $150,000 per year simply by removing one of two glasses on its dinner trays. You can see why airlines often drop features like hot towels or glassware in tougher financial times. Many airlines have cut meal services altogether on flights shorter than three or four hours.

Of course, every item that gets loaded onto an airplane has to be unloaded, sorted, cleaned, recycled, or disposed of (usually by incineration). Statistics on waste are hard to come by, but in 1993 one very large catering company estimated that over 40 percent of its in-flight meals were uneaten or partially eaten. It also recorded disposing of 24 tons of stale bread, 5.7 tons of used frying oil, and 2.5 tons of Styrofoam. Los Angeles International Airport, which dumps about 8,000 tons of wasted food each year, is exploring a novel program in which the scraps get composted, producing methane gas that is pumped to a power generation plant.

Ultimately, it's simply not possible to create gourmet food when cooking for multitudes. Therefore, if you want to enjoy your food on a flight (or perhaps be fed at all, if your flight is short), remember to stop by a deli on the way to the airport. Even if you bring a few granola bars and some fruit, your meal will be healthier and more fulfilling than anything the airlines could serve you (except perhaps in business or first class).

THE TROUBLE WITH TOILETS

Passengers love to hate airplane lavatories: You stand in a long line in order to step into a small, cramped room, which lights up only after you close the door and lock it. The toilets themselves look like prison bathrooms, and they typically make *a lot* of noise when flushed.

Don't blame Boeing or Airbus for long bathroom lines. Decisions about the number of lavatories on a plane, how large they should be, and what amenities they have are all made by the airline companies. Typically, there's an average of about one toilet for every forty-six passengers in economy class, and one for every eleven seats in first class, but the average Boeing 737 has only one toilet for every sixty-three coach passengers.

Neither Boeing nor Airbus actually constructs the lavatories themselves; like almost everything else inside the cabin, these are modular units designed and manufactured by outside suppliers. Airbus purchases "lavs" from German-based Dasell Cabin Interior, while Boeing uses the Japanese firms Jamco and Yokohama Rubber for their wide-body and narrow-body jets, respectively.

Of course, today's toilets have come a long way since the 1920s and 1930s, when raising the toilet seat would reveal nothing more than a hole to the passing landscape below. Flush toilets made their debut in the ultraelegant Boeing 314 "Clippers" and were slowly refined until 1982, when Boeing introduced the first in-flight vacuum toilet system.

Vacuum toilets are far superior to the old flush types for several reasons.

Couples engaging in in–flight sex is rare, but less rare than you might think. Cramped lavatories may be lacking in atmosphere, but they seem to be a popular spot for gaining entrance to the "Mile High Club." In fact, Virgin Atlantic Airways recently announced plans to retrofit newly introduced baby changing stations in the "lavs" on their aircraft because they keep getting broken. (Virgin has surmised that the damage is more likely due to amorous couples than to oversized babies.)

First, they require very little water—only about eight ounces of water per flush, rather than over a gallon of blue disinfectant in the older toilets. (Water weighs about 8.3 pounds per gallon, so carrying less water means a lighter, more efficient airplane.)

Second, the old toilets emptied into separate holding tanks directly beneath each lavatory, which leaked less-than-pleasant smells. Vacuum systems work by momentarily opening a valve to the outside air, creating a pressure differential that sucks the contents from the toilet bowl (which is lined with a teflon-like substance) through pipes to a holding tank in the back of the airplane at about 100 feet per second. If the aircraft is below 16,000 feet, the pressure difference between the air inside and outside the airplane isn't great enough, so there's a built-in "backup" vacuum-generator. The vacuum systems are lighter, easier to fix, and easier to clean than the flush systems (the holding tank is emptied every time the airplane lands).

Another reason the vacuum toilet systems are generally less smelly is that some lavatory air is sucked out, too. However, on occasion, flight attendants are forced to place coffee packets in the lavatories. (They claim coffee is a natural deodorant.) Or they will pull the sink plunger up for a short time in order to suck out more air. This works partly because the sinks aren't connected to the toilet holding tanks; instead, sink water is sprayed out the back of the aircraft during flight, where it vaporizes. The small nozzle near the tail must be specially heated so that it doesn't freeze up at the extremely cold cruising-altitude temperatures.

Curiously, some passengers dislike the vacuum toilets because they're afraid of being sucked in. Don't worry; the hole is simply too small. It is worth noting, however, that you shouldn't try flushing the toilet while seated. In 2001, a passenger flying across the Atlantic on a Boeing 767 became vacuum sealed to a toilet seat after flushing—mechanics were later able to pry her loose after the aircraft landed.

Whatever you do, don't try to smoke in an airplane toilet or disconnect the smoke detector. These are federal offenses for a reason: In 1973, a Boeing 707 jet had to make an emergency landing outside Paris after a fire was started in one of the lavatories, probably from a disposed cigarette. By the time the airplane landed and a rescue crew could open the airplane, almost all the passengers had died. Ten years later, an electrical fire broke out in a lavatory on a flight from Texas to Canada, and half the passengers and crew were killed.

> To begin their boarding process, the airline announces they will preboard certain passengers. And I wonder, How can that be? How can people board before they board? This I gotta see . . . Then they mention that it's a nonstop flight. Well, I must say I don't care for that sort of thing. Call me old-fashioned, but I insist that my flight stop. Preferably at an airport. Somehow those sudden cornfield stops interfere with the flow of my day . . . As part of the continuing folderol, I'm asked to put my seat-back forward. Well, unfortunately for the others in the cabin, I don't bend that way. If I could put my seat-back forward I'd be in porno movies.
>
> Then they say we'll be "landing shortly." Doesn't that sound like we're going to miss the runway? "Final approach" is not too promising either. "Final" is not a good word to be using on an airplane. Sometimes the pilot will speak up and say, "We'll be on the ground in fifteen minutes." Well that's a little vague . . . Which brings us to terminal. Another unfortunate word to be using in association with air travel. And they use it all over the airport, don't they? Somehow I can't get hungry at a place called The Terminal Restaurant. Then again, if you've ever eaten there, you know the name is quite appropriate."
>
> —George Carlin, NAPALM & SILLY PUTTY

FILL 'ER UP:
AIRPLANE FUEL

Airplanes consume a *lot* of fuel: A typical narrow-body jet will burn about 75 gallons of fuel just taxiing out to the runway and then burn about 800 gallons of fuel per hour while in flight. However, aviation professionals don't talk in terms of gallons, they talk about *pounds of fuel*. Jet fuel, which is basically a form of refined oil like kerosene or paraffin, weighs about 6.7 pounds per gallon, so you (or your calculator) can figure that the airlines load around 5,300 pounds of fuel for each hour the aircraft will be in flight, plus about 1,000 pounds for taxiing to and from the runway. They then add enough fuel to redirect the airplane to an alternate airport and stay in a holding pattern for almost an hour. All told, an aircraft like a Boeing 737 may be carrying between 8,000 and 30,000 pounds of fuel when it takes off.

Larger aircraft carry even more. A Boeing 777 runs through about 2,000 gallons (13,400 pounds) of fuel each hour of flight. The Boeing 747, with four engines carrying an aircraft that weighs as much as 870,000 pounds, burns over a gallon of fuel *every second*, or almost 4,000 gallons (26,800 pounds) of jet fuel per hour.

The Boeing 747, which averages about 6 gallons of fuel per mile flown, or .16 miles per gallon, seems like a real gas hog. However, when you figure that the aircraft is carrying perhaps 200 people, it actually gets over three times better gas mileage *per passenger* than an average single-passenger sport utility vehicle.

Airports are also giant refueling stations. For instance, Denver International Airport has eighteen 3-million-gallon (11-million-liter) storage tanks fed by a dedicated fuel pipeline that can bring more than 90,000 gallons of jet fuel into the airport each hour. Fuel can then be pumped directly to each gate or loaded into tanker trucks and driven out to an airplane. The ground crew attaches a fuel hose to each of the aircraft's tanks (usually located on the bottomside of the wings, and sometimes fuselage), making sure that they attach a grounding wire first, to prevent electrical sparks during refueling. When the hose is turned on, the crew can load the airplane's tanks at about 1,000 gallons (6,700 pounds) per minute. That's like fueling 100 cars at the same time!

Jet fuel is less expensive than automobile gasoline, but it still adds up. For instance, in the United States in 2002, the cost of jet fuel averaged about seventy cents a gallon; that means it costs about $40,000 just to fill a Boeing 747's tanks. Fuel alone makes up about 15 percent of a major airline's operating costs (second only to labor, which averages around 36 percent of an airline's costs). This is why airlines are constantly interested in eking out even a tiny bit more fuel efficiency.

> *If you want to fly somewhere . . . first, you have to stand in line to get a boarding pass. That is to replace the ticket they just sold you. Then you have to stand in line to show your boarding pass. That is to prove you bought the ticket they just took away from you. This lets you stand in line to be checked for bombs. Next, you have to stand in line to give back the boarding pass they just gave you . . . This done, you get to stand in line to get on the plane, which enables you to stand in line to go down the plane.*
>
> —Henry Mintzberg, WHY I HATE FLYING

AIRPORT
SECURITY

In today's security-conscious world, it seems strange that only forty years ago airport security was almost exclusively aimed at stopping smugglers and pickpockets. People would often gather on the tarmac to see family members off on a journey. You could drive to the end of the runway to watch flights take off and land. You could even visit the cockpit during a flight to talk with the pilots. However, an increase in politically motivated hijackings and terrorist bombings in the 1960s quickly changed the security landscape.

In 1972, airlines began searching passengers and their bags, and airports hastily set up metal detectors (called *magnetometers*) based on devices originally used in lumber mills to find pieces of metal inside logs. As you walk through a magnetometer, a large metal coil creates a magnetic field that is affected by any metal you're carrying; a large enough deviance in the field causes an alarm to sound.

Some privacy groups in the United States sued the government, arguing that the use of these machines violated the Fourth Amendment, the protection against illegal searches and seizures. The courts agreed that while this *was* a violation, it *was* acceptable as long as it was limited to searching for weapons and explosives, and as long as it was applied universally to all passengers.

Security Today

Today, both magnetometers and X-ray machines are standard equipment at all airports serving major airlines. X rays are very-high-energy light waves that can't be seen but can actually pass through most solid objects. Because different materials absorb different amounts of X rays, a sensor can quickly identify organic, inorganic, and metal objects inside your closed bags. Trained operators aren't only looking for knives; they also try to recognize organic material that might indicate an explosive substance.

If a bag is too densely packed, or contains a laptop computer (which itself is extremely densely packed), the security officials may want to hand-check the contents or use a *sniffer*—a computerized chemistry lab in a box, which can quickly analyze a swab rubbed on you or your bag and sound an alert if there is even a tiny trace of any explosive chemical.

Note that everything beyond the security checkpoint is X-rayed, including the food and dishes at the airport restaurants, the magazines at the newsstands, and the coffee carts. For a while, some airline employees didn't have to undergo these kinds of checks, but that quickly changed in 1987 after a recently dismissed employee bypassed security by flashing his ID card and snuck a gun onto a flight. (He later shot the pilots and crashed the airplane.)

Similarly, until 2001, it was common practice for some airlines to leave their cockpit doors propped open on long international flights to make it easier for pilots and flight attendants to go in and out. However, it took only weeks after the September 11 terrorist attacks on the World Trade Center and the Pentagon before airlines began to install reinforced cockpit doors, ensure that they were kept closed during flight, and even further restrict what people could bring on board.

In the wake of September 11, governments around the world scrambled to find better methods of securing their commercial aircraft. Many pundits pointed to the paragon of airline security, Israel's El Al airline, which not only uses high-tech devices to scan passengers and their baggage, but interrogates them with a barrage of questions such as "Why do you want to visit Israel?" or "Where did you travel while in the country and who did you visit?" Guards look for any suspicious behavior, from shifty eyes to a wavering voice.

On the other hand, most U.S. airports need to process thousands more passengers than El Al, leading them to rely more heavily on mechanical solutions. For example, airline computer systems flag suspicious passengers, such as those who bought a one-way ticket or who aren't frequent flyers on record with the airline. This has led to some absurd situations, such as infants being carefully searched at the gate while their parents stand by, bewildered. Some airlines, in an attempt to save time and money, are apparently trying to do away with human interaction altogether, offering the chance to print boarding passes at kiosks or even from a secure Web site before leaving for the airport (which are then verified with a quick glance at a photo I.D. before boarding).

Security Tomorrow

Airport security—like scheduling or any of the other extraordinarily complex systems that make up the commerical aviation industry—will never be perfect. After all, nothing ever is. But every year each of these systems becomes a bit safer, a bit more robust, and a bit more precise.

Getting on a plane, I told the ticket lady, "Send one of my bags
to New York, send one to Los Angeles, and send one to Miami."
She said, "We can't do that!" I told her, "You did it last week!"
—Comedian Henny Youngman

While passengers grimace at the idea of airplane food, and tremble at the idea of turbulence, when it comes to the treatment of airline luggage, people tend to follow the old adage "If I didn't laugh, I'd cry." Of course disappearing luggage is no joke when it happens to you, and recently the number of complaints filed about baggage being lost or damaged has even surpassed that of complaints about delays. So what actually happens to your bags when you hand them off at the ticket counter or curbside check-in?

Moving Bags

Once you entrust your precious cargo to an airline representative, he or she attaches to it a tag that contains a ten-digit code plus a bunch of information about you and your travel routing: airlines, flight numbers, transfer cities, destination, and so on. This usually appears in both human-readable text and computer-readable bar codes. If your bag or box is particularly heavy, the airline may charge you an overweight baggage fee (because the heavier the airplane, the more fuel it burns).

Then the bag is placed on a conveyor belt, and it disappears from your sight.

Your luggage now enters a race to get to the right airplane at the right time. In most airports around the world, airline employees read each tag individually, heft bags from the primary conveyor belt onto the appropriate cart, drive the cart to the appropriate airplane, and then load the bags onto a conveyor belt leading into the aircraft's cargo hold where other employees place the bags securely. In large wide-body aircraft, baggage handlers first load the cargo into one of several enclosed, metal cargo palettes that are then rolled into the belly of the airplane and locked down for the flight.

However, some airports are so large and handle so much baggage that it's impractical to rely on humans to haul everything from place to place. For example, the San Francisco International Airport alone handles more than 60,000 bags each day. Large airports like this one have computerized luggage-moving systems that rely on a complex series of conveyor belts and chutes.

In this kind of system, your bag's tag is first scanned by a set of laser-beam bar code readers surrounding the primary conveyor belt, similar to the ones at supermarkets. About 10 percent of the time, the tag is folded or otherwise unreadable, and a high-speed mechanical pusher arm immediately shoves the bag to another conveyor to get scanned by hand. Either way, from this moment, the bag is constantly tracked from place to place by hundreds of networked computers, which are also aware of your itinerary and the schedules of every airplane at the airport.

It's not surprising that bags get scratched and scuffed. As they trundle along, they encounter a series of large metal pushers, each of which can shove as many as eighty bags per minute from one conveyor belt to another at just the right moment. Finally, a robotic arm pushes your bag down a chute, where someone loads it onto a truck destined for your flight. If the system's timing is off, your bag ends up on the wrong truck, and then the wrong airplane.

Some huge airports, like Denver International, have done away with the handloading of trucks altogether, and each bag drops from a chute into a moving destination-coded vehicle (DCV)—a small rail cart that travels along miles of twisting underground tracks at almost 20 mph (32 km/hr). The DCV never stops rolling along its mazelike tracks; it simply tips its open-topped bin over at precisely the right moment to receive a bag (one bag per DCV), tips it back up while in transit, and then tips again at the correct moment to drop the bag out at its destination.

Successful luggage-handling systems move your bags at almost exactly the same speed that you move through the airport, so bags don't arrive too late to make your flight or too early—perhaps making a connecting flight that you don't.

> Everyone knows you shouldn't bring explosives or hazardous chemicals on board an aircraft. But did you know mercury is prohibited? Mercury causes aluminum (which many airplanes are made of) to corrode, almost like dry rot in wood. If you drop mercury on the floor of an airplane, it will spread around and a large portion of the fuselage may have to be scrapped. Mercury in a barometer or a personal thermometer is usually allowed if it is entirely enclosed in a protective case.

Being Careful

Along the way to the airplane, your bags are also scanned for contraband such as drugs and explosives. While some airports outside the United States still only X-ray bags, American airports are now employing trained "sniffer" dogs, X-rays, and devices based on computed tomography (CT) scanners, like those in hospitals. Each minute, these devices build "slice" images of about nine pieces of luggage and then automatically compare them to the CT properties of known explosives. The devices can fog your photographic film (even inside lead bags), so most professional photographers carry their film in clear plastic bags and ask that they get hand-checked at the security gate. (The X-ray machines at the passenger security checkpoints are much less powerful, and typically only fog film after many passes.)

However, if the machine does find anything suspicious, the bag gets automatically transferred to another location for a more detailed search, usually done by hand with you watching.

Also, ever since terrorist bombings in the 1980s, airlines are hesitant to allow a passenger's bag to fly without the passenger on board, too. If someone checks in a bag but never boards the aircraft, the airline may pull that bag off before takeoff. Some airlines are taking this process further, giving the baggage handlers handheld bar code scanners that can wirelessly communicate with the central computer to compare each bag with each passenger's boarding status.

> Someday airlines will offer time travel. You can go to the future year 2090 to visit your progeny, but your luggage will wind up in the Middle Ages.
>
> —Frank Romano, technology columnist

While 99.5 percent of bags arrive on the same aircraft as their owners, in 2001, there were 2.2 million reports of mishandled (lost or damaged) luggage in the United States, for an average of 4.55 pieces of luggage per 1,000 passengers. Some airlines tend to track people's bags better than others—Alaska Airlines, for instance, averages less than half the national rate. The good news is that 80 percent of lost bags are retrieved successfully within a day, and 99 percent arrive at their proper destination within five days.

Lost Luggage

With all that computerized technology, how could anything go **worng?** Obviously, in the real world the system is never perfect; tags are misread, bags are routed to the wrong airplanes, and some luggage is simply lost in the shuffle. It's not uncommon for a cart driver to take a corner too quickly and have one or two bags fall off onto the tarmac. In an automated system, an odd-sized bag may fall off a conveyor belt and have to be later retrieved by hand.

Because most luggage mishandling occurs when bags are transferred from one airplane to another, the best way to avoid losing your bags is to fly nonstop. Of course, that's rarely practical these days, so here are a few more tips:

▼ Make your luggage really stand out. Paint fluorescent colors on the side or tie on colored bands. (Use a color other than red, which is overused.) Or perhaps just buy brightly colored bags; they're not fashionable, but they're hard to miss.

▼ Always remove extraneous tags before checking your bag; they might confuse the bar code readers.

▼ Check in an hour or more before your flight, and make sure you have at least an hour layover between flights when connecting, especially when transferring from one airline to another.

▼ Hold on to your claim checks (they're usually stapled to your boarding pass) until you have your bags back. You will need them if anything goes wrong.

▼ Personalize your luggage. You'd be surprised at how many people take home a bag that turns out to be someone else's. Be sure that your name and address are on a tag or label on the outside of the bag, preferably where it cannot be torn off accidentally. Also, put more identifying information (perhaps even your itinerary) inside each bag.

▼ When you check in your bag, make sure to confirm your final destination with the airline representative. Is it San Jose, California (airport code: SJC), or San José, Costa Rica (airport code: SJO)? If you're transferring from one airline to another, or making a connection in a different country from your origin, your bags may only be checked to the intermediate point.

▼ Don't lock your bags or put valuables in them. Security personnel sometimes need to search through checked baggage. Consider packing objects you don't want touched in clear plastic bags. Also avoid packing food or drinks in your bags, as organic items may be flagged as suspicious.

Finally, don't put anything irreplaceable in your checked bags. Only about .005 percent of bags are permanently lost, but that's still enough that you should be wary. Airlines in the United States don't have to pay you more than about $1,250 if they lose your bag on a domestic flight. (You may have to prove the value of the contents.)

International conventions, however, state that airlines only have to pay $9.07 per pound (or $20/kg) for bags lost on international flights—that's about $180 for a twenty-pound bag! The courts have upheld this limit, even in a case where an airline lost a professional courier's bag containing $2 million in cash. Fortunately, you can often buy "excess valuation" insurance when you check in (but even this wouldn't have covered the unfortunate courier's loss).

Carry-on Baggage

Since you shouldn't put your valuables in checked baggage, you'll need to carry them on board with you. Here, too, the airlines have detailed restrictions, such as the maximum size and weight of your carry-on bags. Note that different airlines and different countries have different restrictions; for instance, you may be allowed to bring a bag aboard on the long flight to Australia and later have to check it in on domestic flights within the continent.

The U.S. Federal Aviation Administration provides a list of items you shouldn't carry on board with you (see www.theflyingbook.com for a link to the FAA Web site), including: pepper spray, drain cleaners, bleach, house paint, solvents, hairspray (containers bigger than sixteen ounces), strike-anywhere matches (a small number of regular matches are okay), or sharp objects like knives, scissors, corkscrews, and disposable razor blades. Most likely, the items will just be confiscated, but you can actually be slapped with a hefty fine for each violation if you're found to be willfully breaking the law.

It seems obvious, but you can't carry firearms or ammunition on board. (Every now and again people will honestly forget that they have a gun in their bag; don't be one of them.) You can pack an unloaded firearm in your checked baggage, but you *must* declare it when you check in.

One of the most frequently asked questions at security checkpoints is whether the X-ray machine will damage data on disks and laptops. X rays don't hurt digital media at all, but magnetic fields do. Fortunately, the X-ray machines in most Western airports are well shielded from stray magnetic fields created by their motors, so you don't have to worry. In eastern Europe and developing nations, it may be worth ensuring that these items are checked by hand instead. By the way, the metal-detection devices (magnetometers) that you walk through do create a magnetic pulse, so take that floppy disk out of your pocket.

One more tip: It's worth keeping your carry-on bags locked or at least difficult to open, especially on long international flights. Some unscrupulous people make a living stealing from carry-ons while the airplane is dark and most passengers are asleep. It is also not unheard of for people to slip drugs *into* another passenger's carry-on bag to better the chances of getting them through customs (only to be stolen back later).

DEREGULATION AND TICKET PRICES

Do you long for the "old days" when every seat on an airplane sold for the same amount, and that amount was based on how far you flew? Today, airline ticket prices fluctuate daily—sometimes even hourly—so that you may pay more than $1,000 more for your ticket than the person next to you, or you may pay twice as much to travel 500 miles as you would to travel 3,000 miles. These gross inconsistencies may leave you feeling that the airlines are being unfair in their pricing (unless you're the one with the lower-priced ticket). But fear not; the airlines *are* being consistent. They're consistently trying to make as much money as they can. This chapter describes the situation in the United States.

A Short History Lesson

Between 1934 and 1978, airline fares in the United States were strictly regulated by the government's Civil Aeronautics Board (CAB). The CAB didn't set ticket prices, but airlines were not allowed to change their airfares without the board's permission. While the CAB would let airlines raise fares to cover costs, it rarely let an airline reduce its fares. Not only couldn't the airlines compete based on fares, but the CAB stopped airlines from entering certain markets, fearing that excessive competition would be bad for the American public. The result was high ticket prices, so only business travelers and relatively wealthy people could fly.

Regulation did have its benefits, though. The CAB insisted that airlines fly direct routes between cities, even if those routes weren't popular and the airplanes had to fly less than half full. Also, the airfares were based on the distance between the cities, so flying from San Francisco to New York was more or less the same price as flying from San Francisco to Hartford, Connecticut.

> If we went into the funeral business, people would stop dying.
> —Martin R. Shugrue, vice-chairman of Pan Am, describing how bad business was before the airline went out of business in 1991

> If God wanted us to fly, He would have given us tickets.
> —Comedian Mel Brooks

Since airlines couldn't change their fares, they had to offer other incentives. In the 1950s and early 1960s, airlines tried to sell seats based on how fast they could fly. Advertising "we get you there faster," they pushed their new jet airliners at full throttle. Unfortunately, they soon found that it was an incredibly inefficient use of fuel to fly any faster than about Mach .85 (about 560 mph or 910 km/h). So in the 1960s, airlines began to compete based on better service. Some installed piano lounges and encouraged passengers to sit around large circular tables; others made their young female flight attendants wear sexy uniforms.

Deregulation

By the 1970s, airlines began lobbying the government to dismantle the air travel regulations and let them compete in any way they saw fit, including setting their own airfares. They insisted that unregulated airline travel would be good for the public, pointing toward the great success of a small "discount fare" operation called Southwest Airlines, which had avoided federal regulations by flying only within the state of Texas. By 1978, they had won their argument with Congress, and President Jimmy Carter signed the Airline Deregulation Act into law that year.

As strange as it seems, airlines regularly sell more tickets for some flights than there are seats available. They do this on purpose because a surprising number of people don't show up to flights for which they have a reservation or ticket. Some business passengers book multiple flights near the same time, in case one gets canceled or they're running late. Other passengers simply don't make it to the gate in time. In fact, some estimates suggest that about *half* of all reservations are canceled or turn into no-shows, and as many as 15 percent of the seats on a fully booked flight would go empty if the airline didn't overbook. When too many people do show up, it can be expensive for the airline, but in the long run the company still comes out ahead.

Since then, a number of interesting changes have taken place. First, air fares tumbled drastically on heavily traveled routes, like the one from New York to Chicago. On the other hand, air fares increased on lesser-traveled routes, even when they cover short distances, such as from Los Angeles to Santa Barbara. So while the average price per mile is now significantly lower than it used to be (leading more people than ever to travel by air), passengers outside major metropolitan areas often have to pay more for less service.

In 1978, many people prophesized that the relatively safe airline industry would become dangerous in the postderegulation era, because airlines would cut their safety standards as they cut their airfares. Surprisingly, air travel has actually become safer since deregulation; equipment failures and human errors have all decreased, while air travel has dramatically increased.

Less clear, however, is the question of whether competition has actually increased or decreased. There is fierce competition for major routes like the one from New York to London. But there is often little or no competition at other airports. Some small airports that were once served by several airlines now have only one to choose from—and passengers must pay whatever that airline demands. Other larger airports have become hubs for one or two particular airlines. For instance, it's difficult to fly out of Minneapolis, Minnesota, unless you fly on Northwest Airlines, which owns almost all the gates.

Competition in the United States has also decreased in the past quarter century as six of the eleven major airlines that existed in 1978 have either gone out of business or merged with other companies: Braniff, Eastern, National, Pan American, TWA, and Western. Of the twenty-six regional airlines that formed after World War II—like PSA, Piedmont Airlines, and Flying Tigers Cargo—only US Airways still exists (though it has filed for bankruptcy at

Average Price to Fly Round-trip from Seattle to Los Angeles:		
Year	Price	Price Adjusted for Inflation
1936	$113	$1,354
1958	$97	$559
1970	$142	$609
2002	$260	$260

the time of this writing). Today, fewer than ten airlines control almost every route in the United States.

As it turns out, one of the main factors deciding an airline's fate was how smart it was about pricing its tickets.

Perishable Inventory

To understand how airplane tickets are priced, you have to realize that airline seats are as perishable as fruit in a grocery store. Airlines can only make money when they fill seats on airplanes, and the moment an airplane takes off, any seat that isn't filled is a missed opportunity, like a pear becoming spoiled before it's sold. To maximize profits, the airline needs to fill the airplane while charging as much as it can for each seat. But it knows that it can't fill airplanes by charging full fare.

The trick, then, is to find the balance between filling the airplane with discount air fares (which probably wouldn't generate enough revenue to make the trip profitable) and selling only a portion of the plane's seats at full fare. Airlines know they can charge a business traveler more than the average tourist is willing to pay. They know that people who purchase tickets two days before a flight are more desperate than people who bought them a month earlier. They know that at certain times of the year some travel destinations are more popular than others.

So airlines use all this information to maximize their profits. They offer lower-cost incentives to get people to fly during less popular times (such as Tuesdays and Wednesdays). They charge lower fares to fly into a lesser-used airport like Baltimore's, which is an hour outside Washington, D.C. They offer incentives to buy less flexible, nonrefundable tickets that are purchased as far in advance as possible. They may offer an incentive to stay over a Saturday night, which is unattractive to business fliers.

This explains why a business executive who needs to be on a certain flight the next day will be charged an enormous rate while someone surfing the Internet for good deals can get on the same flight for a fraction of the cost. By agreeing to fly on any flight at any hour, the surfer is a prime target for cheap fares that will fill soon-to-perish seats.

Note that large airlines also use incredibly complex "yield management" software to constantly track and analyze the demand for tickets and compare it to historical data. If one flight starts to sell faster than expected, the software raises the price of the tickets. If another flight is selling slower than it has in the past, the computer may lower the price to encourage more sales. These changes are often made on a daily basis, and sometimes even multiple times each day. When the airlines tell you that a ticket's price is not guaranteed until you buy it, they really mean it!

This kind of analysis can occasionally create bizarre situations where it is actually less expensive to fly a long distance, with one or more stopovers, than it would be to fly directly to one of those stopover cities. Nevertheless, over time these sorts of schemes have increased revenues by at least 7 or 8 percent, and they are now used by hotels, car rental agencies, and other companies that have similar "use it or lose it" inventories.

Answers to Common Air–Travel Questions

(From a piece by Dave Barry originally published in the *Miami Herald*, June 12, 1998)

Q. Airline fares are very confusing. How, exactly, does the airline determine the price of my ticket?

A. Many cost factors are involved in flying an airplane from Point A to Point B, including distance, passenger load, whether each pilot will get his own pilot hat or they're going to share, and whether Point B has a runway.

Q. So the airlines use these cost factors to calculate a rational price for my ticket?

A. No. That is determined by Rudy the Fare Chicken, who decides the price of each ticket individually by pecking on a computer keyboard sprinkled with corn. If an airline agent tells you that they're having "computer problems," this means that Rudy is sick, and technicians are trying to activate the backup system, Conrad the Fare Hamster.

Rules for Frequent Fliers

—An anonymous Internet posting

1. No flight ever leaves on time unless you are running late and need the delay to make the flight.

2. If you're running late for a flight, it will depart from the farthest gate within the terminal.

3. If you arrive very early for a flight, it inevitably will be delayed.

4. Flights never leave from Gate #1 at any terminal in the world.

5. If you work on your flight, you'll experience turbulence as soon as you touch pen to paper . . . or start to drink your coffee.

6. If you're assigned a middle seat, you can determine who has the seats on the aisle and the window while you're still in the boarding area: Just look for the two largest passengers.

7. Only passengers seated in window seats ever have to get up to go to the lavatory.

8. The crying baby on board your flight is always seated next to you.

9. The best-looking woman/man on your flight is never seated next to you.

10. The less carry-on luggage space available on an aircraft, the more carry-on luggage passengers will bring aboard.

The ability of the military's Stealth aircraft to avoid detection is so good that mechanics have reported finding dead bats on the concrete around the airplanes each morning.

When you read about an airplane called the *B-17G* you can tell it's a bomber because of military naming conventions that have been around since 1924. *B-17G* stands for the seventh (G) variant of the seventeenth model of bomber. (No, *B* doesn't mean "Boeing"!) Similarly, *C* means "cargo aircraft," *H* means "helicopter," *K* means "tanker," *R* means "reconnaissance," and *X* means "special research." Today, *F* means "fighter" (like the F–18), but prior to 1947, *F* meant "foto" reconnaissance airplane. So fighters in World War II used *P* (for pursuit).

British
airways
Concorde

seat
7B

seat
no smoking cabin

Royal First Class boarding pass

Name

Flight TG0740

Boarding
Time 095

Class P

Gate

Destn DFW

Seat 03B

Date 16SEP

BUILDING AIRPLANES

The modern automobile is a beautiful piece of machinery, carefully assembled out of several thousand parts. But cars can hardly hold a candle to the astonishing complexity of jet airplanes, which are built from up to 3 million separate parts held together by another 3 million rivets, bolts, and other fasteners. If you've ever wondered about what it takes to build and maintain these behemoths, you'll find the answer right here.

MAKING
AIRPLANES

It's not hard to build an airplane that can fly; in fact, you can even buy a kit and build one at home. What *is* difficult, however, is building an airplane that can fly more than a handful of people safely, economically, with an extremely low rate of parts failure, and with multiple redundant systems for the inevitable times that something does go wrong.

That's one reason there are so few commerical airplane manufacturers in business these days; dozens of aircraft companies have either merged, been bought out, or gone out of business in the pursuit of building successful airplanes. Today, just two companies—Boeing and Airbus—build about 99 percent of large passenger jets (aircraft that carry more than 110 people). The market of smaller regional aircraft companies is only slightly larger, including Embraer (based near São Paulo, Brazil), Saab (based in Sweden), and Bombardier Aerospace (based near Montreal, Canada), which now owns Learjet, de Havilland, and Canadair.

Putting It Together

Each day, fifteen railcars full of airplane parts roll into the Boeing manufacturing plant in Everett, Washington, just north of Seattle. It's here that the Boeing twin-aisle, wide-body aircraft—the 747, 767, and 777—are built inside the world's largest building (measured by volume): one-third of a mile wide and over two-

Opposite: The Everett manufacturing plant.

thirds of a mile long, standing eleven stories tall. You could fit Disneyland inside it and still leave room for fifty acres of indoor parking lots. It takes a lot of power to build big jets: The Everett plant uses as much electricity each year as 32,000 homes.

Everett and its sister plant thirty miles south in Renton, Washington (where Boeing builds the single-aisle 737 and 757 aircraft), assemble their airplanes out of parts made by almost 3,000 suppliers in every one of the fifty American states and sixty-five countries around the world. To make a Boeing 747, it takes about six million individual parts—half of which are rivets, bolts, and other fasteners. A Boeing 737 is much simpler, containing only about 360,000 parts and 600,000 fasteners.

Of course, many of these parts are already pre-assembled when they roll in. For instance, the entire fuselage for the Boeing 737 is built in Wichita, Kansas, before being loaded on a train for its 1,800-mile journey to Renton. The fuselage is so long that before the first one could be shipped, Boeing had to build a wooden mockup and an eighty-nine-foot-long railcar to test whether it would make it cross-country without being damaged in sharp turns or low tunnels. The mockup made it just fine until the rail spurs entered the Renton plant; there Boeing realized that two feet had to be shaved off the side of a factory building. Later, the company encountered one other problem with this transport system: A fuselage would occasionally arrive in Renton with a few small (and easily patched) bullet holes apparently made by locals taking potshots at the train along the way. Security was quickly tightened and this is no longer a concern.

The hollow fuselage takes about six months to build, but once it enters the factory, workers have about eighteen days to attach the wings and tail; line the interior with thirty-six miles of wiring, insulation, and padding; and install the cockpit instruments, nose radar cone, landing gear, interior fixtures (including seats, lavatories, sound-absorbent insulation, and overhead compartments), and engines. Although the aircraft are enormous, the precision is extraordinary: New laser-guided tools can align the wing to the fuselage within a thousandth of an inch.

Airbus Industries assembles its aircraft in a similar way. Sections are built in Germany, Spain, the United Kingdom, and France, and then delivered to Toulouse, France, or Hamburg, Germany, for final assembly and testing. However, Airbus does use a different delivery system to move parts around. Instead of the train, Airbus uses the world's largest civil freight aircraft, its own A300-600ST Super Transporter—nicknamed "Beluga"—which can carry an entire airplane fuselage or a pair of aircraft wings.

Almost everything that you see inside an airplane—lavatories, kitchen galleys, seats, fabrics, and dividers—was ordered by the airline separately from the aircraft itself. Airlines decide seat sizes and configuration, entertainment options (video, telephone, and so on), and even the number and placement of lavatories. Boeing or Airbus may or may not install these items for the airline, depending on the contract.

While aluminum has long been the primary material for building airplanes (it's lightweight and relatively strong), synthetic materials called *composite* are increasingly attractive to aircraft manufacturers. Some carbon-based composites are significantly lighter and stronger than aluminum, and they don't corrode like metal. Today, much of the tail assembly on the Boeing 777 and parts of the wings and tail on some Airbus aircraft are made from composites.

When all the fuel is drained out of a Boeing 747, a person five foot, eight inches (1.7 meters) tall can stand upright inside the wing near where it attaches to the fuselage.

The A300-600ST Beluga-Super Transporter.
(Courtesy of Airbus Industrie)

Finishing Touches

Take a drive through the city of Renton, and you'll see a line of silvery green 737s and 757s on the tarmac of the municipal airport, waiting for paint and flight testing. The greenish color is a vinyl coating, applied before assembly, that protects the metal from corrosion and scratches; it get washed off just before the airplane is given its livery (painted in the colors and style of whatever airline ordered it).

Boeing generally paints an aircraft only once—immediately after it's built—and airlines are responsible for repainting their aircraft from then on. However, Boeing makes an exception for the two modified 747s owned by the U.S. government that fly the president and vice president around (whichever one the president is on at any given moment is called Air Force One), which it repaints every few years.

Painting an airplane isn't like painting a house. The metal skin of the plane is given a slight negative electrical charge and the paint is sprayed on with a slight positive charge so that the paint adheres as smoothly and lightly as possible. Remember, paint adds weight. Jet airplanes typically carry between 400 and 1,000 pounds of paint, which can take three to five days to apply.

Every component of an airplane (every wire, every instrument, and so on) is tested before it rolls off the assembly line. The testers pump air into the cabin to ensure it can withstand twice the amount of pressure it will actually experience in

When Boeing first designed the 777, it offered airlines an option for wings that could fold upward when parked at the gate, like those on navy aircraft carrier jets. This feature would save valuable airport space, but would add to the weight and operating costs of the airplane, so no airline has (to date) asked for it.

On a Boeing 777, the horizontal stabilizers on the tail are small compared to the wings, but these stabilizers are as big as the main wings on a Boeing 737. Each engine on a 777 is as wide as the fuselage on a Boeing 727.

The Boeing Company was founded in 1916, and over the years it has built high-tech hydrofoils, airplane engines, and even the lunar rover. However, when finances were tight, the company manufactured railcars, boats, and even furniture.

Everyone knows that the two largest commercial jet airliner companies today are Boeing and Airbus. Here's the geneaology of some other important airplane manufacturers.

The Glenn L. Martin Company (founded in 1912) merged with American-Marietta Corporation in 1961 to create Martin–Marietta, which in 1995 merged with Lockheed Corporation (originally founded in 1916 as the Loughead Aircraft Manufacturing Company) to form Lockheed Martin. Lockheed built the famous L–1011 "TriStar" wide–body jet in 1972.

Douglas Aircraft Company (founded in 1920) and the McDonnell Aircraft Company (founded in 1939) merged in 1967 to form McDonnell–Douglas. The last Douglas–designed passenger aircraft, the DC–10, rolled out in 1970. All subsequent designs had the "MD" moniker, such as the MD–80, which was originally to be the DC–9 "Super 80." Boeing acquired McDonnell–Douglas in 1997, and the MD–90 aircraft was given a new name, the Boeing 717.

flight. Even the landing gear is raised and lowered numerous times while the airplane is jacked up in the factory. Nevertheless, before delivery to an airline, each aircraft is also given two or more test flights by trained test pilots from both the manufacturer and the airline. A new wide-body jet costs well over $150 million, and repairs aren't cheap either, so airlines are extremely careful that the aircraft is in perfect flying condition when they assume ownership.

Besides, the airlines don't waste time and money by taking a new jet home to admire it. Instead, they often fly it directly from the factory to an airport to pick up passengers.

The airline manufacturing industry relies on a "just in time" inventory system. For example, the jet engines for a Boeing 777 cost about $15 million each, so Boeing does not just have piles of them sitting around. Instead, they arrive at the last stages of the aircraft assembly, just in time to be tested and installed.

When the Boeing 747 was first designed in the late 1960s, no one was sure whether the world wanted an airplane that big. True, flying was beginning to become the popular way to travel, and between 1960 and 1966 the number of air passengers nearly doubled to 200 million. But Boeing took an enormous risk, literally betting the future of the company on the success of this aircraft. Pan American Airlines only agreed to buy the first twenty-five 747 aircraft on the condition that Boeing could prove that the airplane would be profitable even if it were only flown with cargo. Fortunately, the 747 became immensely successful flying both cargo and passengers, and today it is the most recognized aircraft in the world.

Here are a few statistics on this famous airplane. (Note that most of the following refers to the Boeing 747-400, which is the only model Boeing currently builds, but which is significantly different from the early models, such as the -100 and the -200.)

The Boeing 747-100 was first flown in 1969. The first passenger flight, from New York to London, was on January 21, 1970. The one millionth passenger flew on a 747 six months later on July 16, 1970.

Most passenger 747s in service today are the 747-400 model:

First entered service in 1989.

Length: 231 feet, 10 inches (70.6 meters)

Wingspan: 211 feet, 5 inches (64.4 meters)

Height of tail: 63 feet, 8 inches (19.4 meters)

Width of interior cabin: 20 feet (6.1 meters)

Maximum takeoff weight: 875,000 pounds (396,890 kg)

Maximum fuel load: 57,285 U.S. gallons (or 383,800 pounds, 216,840 l)

Maximum range: 7,325 nautical miles (8,430 statute miles, or 13,570 km)

Typical takeoff speed: 160 knots (180 mph or 290 km/h)

Typical takeoff distance: 10,500 feet (about 2 miles or 3.2 km)

Typical cruise speed: .85 Mach (565 mph or 910 km/h)

Typical landing speed: 140 knots (160 mph or 260 km/h)

Boeing offers three types of 747s: all-passenger, passenger and cargo (called *combi*), and all-cargo. An average two-class passenger configuration carries 524 passengers; the average three-class configuration carries 416 passengers. In the combi and cargo configurations, the nose can be fitted as a door to facilitate the loading of long and bulky articles.

The flight deck has 365 lights, gauges, and switches (reduced from 971 on earlier 747 models).

There are about 171 miles (274 km) of wiring inside a 747.

Covering about 5,600 square feet (525 m²), the wings cover a greater area than a basketball court. Each wing weighs 28,000 pounds (12,700 kg).

The 747-400 has a flexible cabin interior: Seats, class configurations, galleys, and even lavatories can be moved within one or two days.

Over 1,215 Boeing 747s have been built; about 1,100 are still in service.

Boeing 747s have flown over 2.2 billion passengers in the past thirty years.

On the average international 747 flight, an airline must load over 50,000 in-flight service items and 5.5 tons of food.

Like a tree flexing in the wind, the wingtips are designed to bend over 10 feet up or down.

The 747 carries half of all air freight flown worldwide.

The U.S. Postal Service unveiled its thirty-three-cent postage stamp commemorating the 747 in 1999.

Each of the four engines can produce about 60,000 pounds of thrust

The Boeing 747 has five wheel trucks: one in the front of the aircraft, one under the base of each wing, and two under the airplane's belly. The nose truck has two wheels, while each other truck has four wheels with nonskid, high-pressure tires that can bear almost 425,000 pounds. Safety regulations require that the plane can land safely on only two of the four rear trucks.

AIRCRAFT MAINTENANCE

The airplane you next fly on might be twenty, thirty, or even forty years old. Does that make you nervous? After all, you can hardly expect to drive 1,000 miles in a vintage 1970 car without a breakdown or two. But if you treated your car as well as airlines treat their airplanes, you could probably drive it your entire life.

A big commercial jet receives about eleven hours of maintenance for every hour it flies. Smaller commuter airplanes, with their simpler designs and systems, may receive only six hours for each hour of flight. No, airplanes don't break down that often; it's simply that airlines are heavily invested in making sure their aircraft are always in peak operating condition. Low-level mechanical problems can mean lower fuel efficiency, which can quickly become expensive. (Airlines in the United States alone consume over 10 billion gallons (38 billion liters) of fuel each year; a difference of even 1 percent in efficiency is a matter of millions of gallons.) Of course, more serious mechanical problems cause delays or even accidents, which are extremely expensive, or even disastrous, for the airline.

Each commercial airplane has its own maintenance schedule, based on a certain number of hours in flight and *cycles* (takeoffs and landings). Mechanics inspect every aircraft at least once each day, looking for obvious problems and giving special attention to concerns logged by the pilots and flight crew (called *squawks*). If any repairs are needed to an item on the airplane's official *minimum equipment list*, the airplane may be kept longer. Then, every six or seven days, two mechanics give the aircraft a more thorough review (sometimes called an *A Check*), which can usually be performed overnight.

Once every month or so, the aircraft gets a *B Check*, in which between ten and forty mechanics look over every major system (hydraulics, electrical, brakes, and so on). Then, every eighteen to twenty-four months, the maintenance crew takes the airplane out of service for ten to forty-five days for an even closer inspection. If that weren't enough, every four years or so, the airline pulls out all the seats and many of the interior fixtures in order to check the fuselage for signs of stress or other wear and tear. And after eight or nine years, the mechanics tackle the biggest job of all: They strip the entire airplane down—literally taking apart every system in the aircraft, including the engines—check every item, and then put it all back together again.

Plus, you might think your mechanics down at "Heinrich's Auto" are good, but did the person who checked your brakes have to pass a federal certification exam? Did she precisely follow written procedure and then document the work in detail, including noting the serial number of every part she replaced? Airline maintenance has gotten a bad reputation in recent years, but the truth is that these mechanics are extremely well trained and are under constant peer and supervisor review.

Airlines are required to keep every page of maintenance paperwork for their airplanes, including pilots' logs and mechanics' checklists—even if nothing was found wrong. That's no small feat, as each year the average commercial aircraft gathers about twelve inches of paperwork.

All commerical aircraft are boarded from the left. Some historians have linked this convention to the custom of mounting horses from the left side (which may have started when soldiers had swords hanging along their left legs). It would be incredibly difficult to change this arrangement because all airports are designed around this configuration.

When you board an airplane, check the little metal registration plate above or on the side of the open door. This plate often tells you what year the airplane was built.

It's no wonder that some estimates place maintenance costs at about $1 million per airplane per year. In fact, while most airplanes are removed from service after about twenty or thirty years, there are still aircraft from the 1930s that are providing safe and efficient commercial service in some places around the world. So next time you read a newspaper article implying that airlines are flying old aircraft, remember that the word *old* is relative.

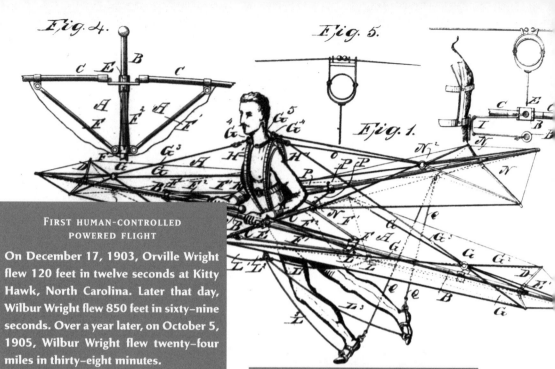

Fig. 4. Fig. 5. Fig. 1.

FIRST HUMAN-CONTROLLED POWERED FLIGHT

On December 17, 1903, Orville Wright flew 120 feet in twelve seconds at Kitty Hawk, North Carolina. Later that day, Wilbur Wright flew 850 feet in sixty-nine seconds. Over a year later, on October 5, 1905, Wilbur Wright flew twenty-four miles in thirty-eight minutes.

FIRST SKYWRITING

Milton J. Bryant first wrote words in the sky over Seattle on July 19, 1913, though which words exactly have been lost over time. However, the first commercial use of skywriting was in May 1922, when Captain Cyril Turner wrote "Daily Mail" over London. (Later that year he wrote "Hello USA" over New York City in an effort to drum up an advertising contract.)

In 1911, thirty-two-year-old Calbraith Perry Rogers became the first person to fly across the American continent. He paid for the trip by naming his airplane after a popular soda: the *Vin Fizz*. During the forty-nine-day journey he crashed at least nineteen times (various sources define *crash* differently; some say he crashed as many as sixty times), and by the end of the flight, he had replaced every part on the airplane except a rudder and one wing strut. Sadly, a year later he was killed after a midair collision with a seagull.

FIRST IN-FLIGHT MOVIE

While there is some controversy over this record, it's likely that the first in-flight movie was the silent film classic *The Lost World* (complete with animated dinosaurs), presented on Britain's Imperial Airways in April 1925, en route from London to Paris.

FIRST GUN FIRED FROM AIRPLANE

Lieutenant Jacob Fickel shot at ground targets on August 20, 1910, from a Curtiss biplane over Sheepshead Bay, New York.

FLYING THROUGH HISTORY

To fly. It is one of humankind's oldest dreams, talked about for millennia by scientists, philosophers, and poets. No other invention fulfilled a dream so long held or so widely considered impossible. Today, with millions of flights each year, it is easy to take flying for granted—as though the mechanics of flight were obvious. So let's take a moment to look at the amazing journey of flight over the past two centuries, as well as three men who were largely responsible for making commercial aviation history possible: Orville and Wilbur Wright, and Charles A. Lindbergh.

A BRIEF HISTORY
OF FLIGHT

For over 4,000 years, everyone who dreamed of flight made a simple and obvious assumption: Since flying animals all have flapping wings that both lift them into the air and propel them forward, a flying machine for humans should try to do this, too. The thirteenth-century Franciscan monk Roger Bacon rightly believed that air could support a craft in the same way that water supports a boat, but he wrote of *ornithopters* that would use birdlike wing motions to keep afloat. In the fif-

The d'Ecquevilly multiplane, 1908.

teenth century, Leonardo da Vinci designed several ornithopters with flapping wings, though it's unclear whether he ever built them. Certainly, they would never have flown if he had.

In fact, it wasn't until 1809 that Englishman Sir George Cayley had a breakthrough idea. Like most breakthroughs, this one was simple: Use one device to move the aircraft forward and another to keep it in the air. The thrust would come from an *airscrew* which, because it propelled the vehicle forward, would later be called a *propeller*. The lift would come from an

Sir George Cayley conceived the idea of the airplane fifty–six years before the invention of the bicycle in 1865. Of course, it was almost a century after Cayley that the Wright brothers actually flew an aircraft with any control.

unmoving *fixed wing*, which would also be called a *plane* (and thus *airplane*). Cayley's insight, radical for the time, changed the course of aviation forever.

Gliding (1800–1900)

There was one problem with Cayley's idea: No one had invented a propulsion system powerful enough yet light enough to be fitted on an aircraft. So Cayley built a fixed-wing glider and enlisted a servant to fly it off a hill. The man lived, but the aircraft didn't. (As Cayley's granddaughter diplomatically noted, "I think it came down in rather a shorter distance than expected.")

Of course, some inventors continued to flap around (on the ground) in ornithopters, but for serious researchers, the rest of the nineteenth century was all about finding the best shape for a wing. A glance at a bird's wing was enough guidance: The top of the wing should be curved so that air passing over it will be deflected downward. However, the exact shape, called an *airfoil*, depended on a number of factors such as the width and length of the wing.

Yet, few inventors were patient enough to figure out the optimal airfoil, and instead simply followed their intuition. Each overexuberant inventor promised that his design would be the first to fly. In fact, two hopeful entrepreneurs named William Henson and John Stringfellow even founded the Aerial Transit Company in 1843 on such promises, though they hadn't built (much less flown) an aircraft.

> *The aeroplane will never fly.*
> —*Lord Haldane,*
> *British minister of war, 1907*

> *Heavier-than-air flying machines are impossible.*
> —*William Thomson (Lord Kelvin),*
> *president, Royal Society, 1895*

Those who were patient, like the Russian Alexander Mozhaiski and the German Otto Lilienthal, made great strides forward. Mozhaiski was perhaps the first person to build an airplane capable of flight, in 1884, but it lacked any real controls and quickly crashed.

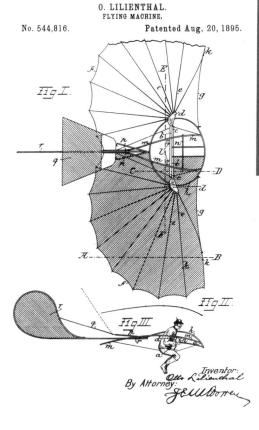

O. LILIENTHAL.
FLYING MACHINE.
No. 544,816.
Patented Aug. 20, 1895.
Fig I.
Fig II.
Fig III
Inventor:
Otto Lilienthal
By Attorney:

The example of the bird does not prove that man can fly. Imagine the proud possessor of the aeroplane darting through the air at a speed of several hundred feet per second. It is the speed alone that sustains him. How is he ever going to stop?

—Mathematician and astronomer Simon Newcomb, in THE INDEPENDENT, *October 22, 1903*

Otto Lilienthal's glider.

Lilienthal understood that it was useless to lift off the ground if you couldn't control the aircraft, so he had a giant hill built outside Berlin for gliding experiments. He took hundreds of flights in his homemade glider (which looked somewhat like a modern hang glider with a tail), slowly becoming proficient at controlling his aircraft and systematically keeping detailed records of his flights. The world learned of Lilienthal's success after French-born Octave Chanute published in 1894 *Progress in Flying Machines,* the same book that inspired two American brothers to take up a new hobby: building an airplane.

Although Lilienthal understood how to glide better than anyone, he insisted that a powered aircraft would require flapping wings and even built two models that never left the ground. Then, on a routine gliding experiment in 1896, the forty-eight-year-old Lilienthal was killed when his glider, caught in a gust of air, stalled and crashed. His tombstone reads *Opfer müssen gebracht werden* (Sacrifices must be made).

Controlled Flight (1900–1916)

By the turn of the century, dozens of people were building airplanes, including Hiram Maxim (the inventor of the machine gun), and Samuel Langley, an influential scientist and the secretary of the Smithsonian Institution in Washington, D.C. Newspapers carried reports almost monthly of someone claiming to have flown, like the little-known Gustave Whitehead who insisted he flew his airplane in Pittsburgh, Pennsylvania, in 1901—unfortunately, without reliable witnesses.

In truth, few designs were even as successful as Langley's 1903 *Aerodrome,* which was catapulted off the top of a houseboat and flew directly into the Potomac River. Langley was so well-known that for several decades the Smithsonian insisted that because Langley's airplane *might* have flown, he should get the credit for inventing the airplane.

Finally, on December 17, 1903, Orville and Wilbur Wright succeeded in flying a controllable, self-propelled aircraft: the *Wright Flyer.* Witnesses took pictures

Glen Curtiss in the JUNE BUG, *July 4, 1908.*

and reported the event, but because the brothers were concerned about obtaining a patent they didn't show their aircraft publicly until August 1908, and then only in Europe. So the first public demonstration of an airplane was on October 23, 1906, in France, by Brazilian inventor Alberto Santos Dumont. The first public demonstration in the United States was performed by Glenn Curtiss a month before the Wright's, on July 4, 1908, in his *June Bug*. Curtiss and the Wright brothers would be involved with patent infringement suits for years to come after this.

While most people today have never heard of Glenn Curtiss, he was perhaps just as important to the success of the early aviation industry as the Wright brothers. He built the first seaplane and later the *Curtiss Jenny* (the JN-4D), which became one of the most popular airplanes of its time.

The Wright brothers first flight at Kitty Hawk, Orville at the controls. **THE FLYER** had no wheels; rather it slid on skids along a wood rail.

Flying exhibitions were extremely popular in these early years. Few people at that time had actually seen an airplane fly, and the general consensus was that flight was simply impossible. As one early pilot, Beckwith "Becky" Havens, noted, "They thought you were a fake, you see. There wasn't anybody there who believed an airplane would really fly. In fact, they'd give odds. But when you flew, oh my, they'd carry you off the field."

Before 1914, however, airplanes were somewhat of a novelty, not particularly useful for anything. But all that changed with the outbreak of World War I.

The Military and Commercial Explosion
(1916–1926)

If the nineteenth century was all about the wing, the twentieth century was all about the engine. The quest for the power to fly faster, longer, and with both cargo and passengers dominated the field of aviation. In 1914 Anthony Jannus piloted the very first scheduled passenger airline service, between the Florida cities of St. Petersburg and Tampa. That sounds more impressive than it was: With only a single passenger and the pilot in an open cockpit, the airplane flew about ten feet above the ground the whole way. The service lasted only three months.

Although several European governments had recognized the military potential of airplanes early on, the United States had surprisingly little interest in aircraft until the outbreak of World War I. Suddenly, the idea of *air superiority* was born, and who controlled the skies could clearly influence who controlled the ground. An enormous effort went into building faster aircraft that could carry guns and bombs.

Then, after the war ended in 1918, governments realized that these aircraft could now be used for civilian purposes. The U.S. Post Office started an experimental airmail route between New York City and Washington, D.C., which was soon expanded cross-country to San Francisco. In 1920, it took seventy-eight hours for airmail to cross the continent, in part because airplanes could not fly reliably in clouds or at night.

This unreliability was due to the fact that no instruments had yet been developed to tell pilots where they were headed. The phrase "flying by the seat of your pants" derived literally from the fact that pilots could only figure out when they were turning, rising, or falling by the sensations they felt against their seat.

> **FIRST FLIGHT AROUND THE WORLD**
> On April 6, 1924, four Douglas DWC World Cruisers took off from Seattle. Only two completed the 26,345-mile journey. Total time actually flying: 371 hours and eleven minutes, at an average flying speed of 75 mph.

Within three years, half of the original forty airmail pilots had been killed in crashes.

While the United States focused on moving the mail, other countries were founding national airlines to move passengers around. By 1926, most European nations had a government-subsidized airline industry, and there were scheduled passenger flights in South America, Australia, and Africa. Of course, flying was a tedious, loud, and dangerous business back then. In fact, taking the train was generally faster and far more comfortable.

Aviation Grows Up (1927–1940)

Certainly, there was some passenger aviation in the United States during the early 1920s. After all, airlines couldn't help but notice the constant stream of American passengers who were trying to accompany the airmail, even if it meant sitting on bags of letters. However, not only was passenger flight prohibitively expensive for most people, but the vast majority of Americans distrusted flying.

Then, almost overnight, Charles Lindbergh's 1927 solo flight across the Atlantic changed American attitudes about flying. After his record-setting flight, Lindbergh traveled around the United States and the world preaching that airplanes were the future of transportation, and people believed him. Of course, only the wealthiest could fly in those days. On the first transcontinental flights in 1929, passengers still flew only by day (they took the train to further their journey at night), and tickets for the twenty-eight-hour trip cost $338 each way (about $7,000 for a round-trip ticket at today's cost).

Nevertheless, these large sums of money did not

In 1934, President Franklin Roosevelt canceled all government airmail subsidies and ordered the military to carry the mail instead. But army pilots were ill prepared for long-distance, scheduled flight. In two weeks, ten pilots died in crashes, and Roosevelt quickly changed his mind.

The twelve-engined, luxurious Dornier Do X, 1929.

buy luxury. The cabin of the ultramodern Ford Trimotor (nicknamed "the Tin Goose") was sweltering in the summer, freezing in the winter, and so loud that passengers had to wear earplugs. Plus, using the toilet was an adventure: Below the seat was simply a hole framing the passing landscape.

Fortunately, in 1933 Boeing released the 247, which many consider to be the first modern airliner. It could fly ten passengers and their luggage almost 500 miles at 155 mph, crossing the United States in only twenty hours. TWA (which was Transcontinental and Western Airlines before it became Trans World Airlines) desperately wanted to buy a Boeing 247, but the early models were all reserved for United Airlines. So TWA commissioned Douglas Aircraft to build an even better airplane; the DC-3, which in 1935 could fly twenty-one passengers across the

Four of the earliest airmail carriers—Varney Air Lines, Boeing Air Transport, National Air Transport, and Pacific Air Transport—banded together in 1934 to form a single company: United Airlines.

The Chinese invented the *airscrew* (*propeller*) over 2,400 years ago but used it solely as a toy that could fly up to fifty feet into the air.

country in greater comfort and in only sixteen hours. The DC-3 was an enormous success: By 1939, 90 percent of the world's airline traffic traveled aboard these aircraft. The DC-3 was so stable, economical, and easy to fix that there are *still* a handful flying in various locations around the world.

Airlines advertised the wonderful views from airplanes (remember that few people had seen the world from any great height before) and used slogans like "Good night, New York . . . Good morning, California!" However, airplanes were still not pressurized, which meant they could not fly above the clouds or above stormy and turbulent weather. It wasn't until 1938, when Boeing introduced the pressurized 307 Stratoliner that passenger flight evolved from being tolerable to being pleasant. Soon after, however, World War II turned the world's aviation industries once again toward the advanced needs of the military. By the end of the war the Boeing 307 was obsolete, as the world had caught its first glimpse of a new propulsion system: The jet engine.

The Jet Age (1940–)

When Frank Whittle invented the jet engine in England during the late 1920s, few people thought it would ever amount to anything. However, Whittle's ideas were finally validated in the summer of 1944, when the first fighter jets flew into service. The jets were faster than anything else in the sky, and they quickly shot down dozens of aircraft. Unfortunately, the jets were the Messerschmitt Me262, and they were flown by the German Luftwaffe against the Allied forces. Fortunately, the Nazis' jets came too late to change the course of the war.

Year	Fastest Airplane	Longest Nonstop Flight	Number of Licensed Pilots in the United States
1919	164 mph (264 km/hr)	1,936 miles (3,115 km)	3,544
1939	365 mph (587 km/hr)	7,162 miles (11,526 km)	31,264
1999	4,520 mph (7,274 km/hr, Mach 6.7)	25,000+ miles (40,000+ km)	750,000+

When World War II ended, hundreds of thousands of soldiers returned to their homes either as experienced pilots or as confident passengers. Multiengine propeller aircraft such as the Lockheed Constellation (later nicknamed "the Connie"), which were originally designed for military cargo, were quickly fashioned for passenger travel. The Connie became very popular and was the first passenger airliner that could fly nonstop across the United States (the journey took about eleven hours with fifty-four passengers).

It didn't take long, however, for airline manufacturers to realize that the future was in jets. The British-built de Havilland Comet, with its four jet engines built directly into the center of the wings (not bolted onto the wings like the engines in most of today's jet airliners), entered service in 1952, and soon every airline was clamoring for a cutting-edge Comet. But in 1954, two extraordinary crashes made it clear that something was terribly wrong with the jet's design. It was only after investigators submerged the fuselage of a Comet in a giant water tank and repeatedly pressurized it and depressurized it that the mystery was solved: metal fatigue. In retrospect, the problem was obvious, but no one had flown an aircraft so often at high altitudes before. The Comet was redesigned and went on to have a safe and successful future.

By the end of the 1950s, the Boeing 707 and Douglas DC-8, both four-engine aircraft with swept-back wings, were convincing passengers that jets could be safe,

FIRST AERIAL REFUELING

On November 12, 1921, Wesley May stepped from the wing of one airplane to the wing of another with a five-gallon can of gasoline on his back.

FIRST NONSTOP FLIGHT ACROSS THE UNITED STATES

John Macready and Oakley Kelly in 1923 flew from New York to San Francisco in twenty-six hours and fifty minutes.

fast, and even economical. The 707 could fly across the United States in under six hours, and from New York to Paris in under nine hours, less than half the time of the fastest propeller airplanes.

Now, flying was no longer reserved for the elite, as companies such as Pan American made it more affordable than ever for families to travel throughout the world. Of course, flying was still a novelty to many people. Not only would folks dress up for the occasion, but—because airport security was nothing like it is today—families often gathered with friends around the aircraft on the tarmac before takeoff.

Boeing had bet the company by developing the 707 (it actually cost more to develop that jet than Boeing's entire net worth at the time), and its success paid off enormously. By the end of the 1960s, the company was ready to bet again, and this time it created the 747. No one knew if people would want to fly on an airplane that big, but Boeing couldn't develop it unless airlines promised to buy the aircraft when it was done. So Pan Am's founder (Juan "Terry" Trippe, whose influence over the aviation industry probably made him the most important person in aviation from the mid-1930s until the end of the twentieth century) made Boeing promise in return that the 747 would be economical to fly as a cargo jet, even without passengers.

If the 747 had failed, Boeing would have gone out of business. Neither Boeing nor Pan Am needed to be concerned; the 747 went on to become incredibly successful, and today it is perhaps the most recognized airplane in the world.

After the incredible leaps forward in aviation during the first seventy years of flight, surprisingly little changed in basic airplane design in the last quarter of the twentieth century. There were, of course, major improvements to onboard safety equipment, such as better navigation equipment and wind shear detectors. Nevertheless, airplanes flew at about the same speed, though over somewhat longer distances and with two engines instead of four. However, the industry evolved in other ways having more to do with the passenger experience.

For instance, there were significant changes in airport and airplane security after terrorist attacks in the early 1970s, and again after the hijackings of 2001. The creation of an economy class and subtle improvements in fuel efficiency made flying less expensive than ever before, and millions more people could now afford to fly. On the downside, much of the special quality of flying was lost as airlines needed to herd more passengers in order to break even financially.

Two hundred years ago, George Cayley made a breakthrough that would enable humans to unveil the mystery of flight. One hundred years ago, the Wright brothers and other aviation pioneers risked their lives determining how to break the bonds of gravity. Today, the airline industry is at a crossroads. How can the present limitations of speed and distance be overcome? How will the often opposing forces of safety and economics play out? How will aviation evolve in the years to come? If the past century has been any indication, this next century will be a fascinating one.

When the multimillionaire Howard Hughes tried to buy a Boeing 307 in 1938 in order to break the round-the-world speed record, he was told that TWA and Pan American Airways had contracts reserving the aircraft. Unfazed, Hughes decided to buy TWA outright. The outbreak of World War II, however, prevented him from ever making the flight.

The Boeing 314, better known as the "Clipper," was the ultimate in luxury, but it wasn't cheap. You could fly on Pan American Airways' Clipper from San Francisco to Manila (in the Philippines) for about $800 each way (about $21,000 round-trip in today's dollars).

If you bring your children in first class, they [should be] required to be strapped to your chest until they're 14.

—Comedian Joan Rivers

THE WRIGHT
BROTHERS

Perhaps the most appropriate word to describe Orville and Wilbur Wright is not *genius,* as some people think, but *chutzpah,* a word developed by Eastern European Jews to signify outrageous persistence and brazen nerve. After all, these two sons of a devoutly religious minister in the U.S. Midwest were not highly educated scientists or aristocrats of great means. They were relatively nondescript Ohio boys who had the gall to follow their dreams.

Wilbur, born in 1867, and Orville, born four years later, had two older brothers and one younger sister. From an early age both were curious about all things mechanical. After high school (neither attended college), Orville became interested in printing and fashioned a basic printing press with which he started a neighborhood newspaper (no small feat). Wilbur had many interests, but no particular vocational plans, and so Orville talked him into being editor of the paper. By 1892 the two had gotten caught up in the new sport of bicycling, and they decided to open a bicycle shop together. Only two years later, they read about Otto Lilienthal's gliding experiments, and the seed of what would become their life's passion was planted.

However, Orville contracted typhoid fever in 1896 (the same year that Lilienthal died in a crash), and it was not until 1899 that the two could begin seriously researching how to build a glider. They read everything available on the subject, even sending away for material from the Smithsonian Institution, and they began to study how birds fly. Slowly the brothers built their glider while still running their bicycle business. They wrote to the U.S. Weather Bureau for suggestions of where the wind blew strongly and steadily. The answer: Kill Devil Hill, near Kitty Hawk, North Carolina.

In September 1900, they made the 750-mile journey from Dayton, Ohio, and found, to their dismay, that the previously published research on which they had based their calculations for their glider design had been flawed. Their glider didn't perform as they had expected, and over the next year they endured many disappointing experiments. By 1901, on the verge of giving up the whole endeavor, Wilbur announced, "Not within a thousand years will man ever fly."

But discovering that previous research is wrong is still an important discovery. With this in mind, the brothers embarked upon two years of slow, painstaking experiments, including using a wind tunnel to rework all of Lilienthal's lift tables. What makes these two bicycle mechanics so impressive in retrospect is that they backed up their *chutzpah* with methodical and often grueling work.

It paid off. In 1902 they made over 1,000 flights on

The Wright brothers in 1910.

> *Learning the secret of flight from a bird was a good deal like learning the secret of magic from a magician. After you know what to look for you see things that you did not notice when you did not know exactly what to look for.*
>
> —Orville Wright

their newly designed glider, patiently learning how to control their craft before deciding to start experimenting with powered flight. The Wrights were probably the first to realize that propellers could be like small rotating wings—that their shape could "lift" the airplane forward as they pushed air back. They also knew the importance of a lightweight engine, and they had one specially built. On December 14, 1903, once again back near Kitty Hawk, Wilbur won a coin toss to see who would fly first. Unfortunately, he had a minor crash immediately upon takeoff, and

Orville Wright was once asked if his life's most exciting moment was that day in 1903 when he first flew. He replied, "No, I got more thrill out of flying before I had ever been in the air at all—while lying in bed thinking how exciting it would be to fly."

it wasn't until December 17 that their airplane, named *The Flyer*, was fixed and ready to take off again.

This time it was Orville's turn, and he took off into a wind blowing at 20 mph. The first controlled, powered flight in history lasted only twelve seconds and covered only 120 feet—shorter than the economy-class section of a Boeing 747 today—but it was proof enough that humankind could fly, something that few people believed was possible at the time.

Soon they were flying farther and longer, but the brothers were afraid others would steal their ideas and so avoided demonstrating their aircraft publicly. Even after receiving a patent, they refused to show their airplane until 1908, when Wilbur flew before a large crowd in France and Orville flew several times at a military base near Washington, D.C. It was on one of these flights that Orville crashed while carrying a passenger, twenty-six-year-old Lieutenant Thomas Selfridge. Orville survived with several broken ribs, but Selfridge died, becoming the first powered airplane fatality.

The Wright brothers, who never married and who lived together with their father and sister, made a fortune by selling aircraft and licensing airplane exhibitions, but also spent much of their time trying to ensure their position as the original inventors of the airplane and suing other manufacturers for patent infringement. They never lost a case, but after Wilbur died from typhoid fever in 1912, Orville lost much of his interest in the aviation business. He eventually sold the Wright Flyer Company and all their patents for $1 million. Orville died at the age of seventy-seven in 1948, having pursued his dream for half a century, and ensured the brothers a place in history.

Opposite: THE FLYER

The Wright brothers may not have been the first to fly a powered aircraft. Two years earlier, in 1901, Gustave White–head built an airplane shaped somewhat like a bat in Bridgeport, Connecticut. Several eyewitnesses reported that Whitehead flew several times, for as far as 1.5 miles. A number of photographs exist of Whitehead and his airplane, but none show him in the air.

LINDBERGH:
THE LONE EAGLE

What son of a U.S. congressman dropped out of college to become a pilot and later won the Pulitzer Prize, the Congressional Medal of Honor, and the first Distinguished Flying Cross? Hint: He worked as an airmail carrier, invented one of the earliest mechanical hearts, and managed to fly fifty fighter combat missions as a civilian during World War II. This extraordinary man was Charles A. Lindbergh (1902–74), and in 1927 he became the world's first media superstar for performing one daring act: flying solo, nonstop, from New York to Paris in thirty-three and a half hours.

This was an extraordinary feat, to be sure, but it's safe to say that Lindbergh's unprecedented celebrity—he was even better known than many of today's sports or pop music stars—resulted as much from his exceptional personal characteristics playing themselves out on the world stage as from his record-breaking flight.

The World Awaits a Hero

In 1927, the United States was bounding from a rural economy to a technological powerhouse, so who could better represent the hopes and dreams of the country than a farm boy with a passion for flying? Perhaps more important, the media had finally developed methods of sending photographs over wire, sound was being married to motion pictures, and the world was becoming networked by cable and radio so that news could quickly spread. The only thing they needed was news.

Eight years earlier, a wealthy French-born hotel owner, Raymond Orteig, had offered a $25,000 prize for the first nonstop flight between New York and Paris. Several well-known pilots attempted the trip; most of them died or were injured in the process. By 1927, advances in engine and airframe reliability had made long distance-flying viable, and suddenly a flock of celebrated aviators vied to snatch the prize. Flyers such as Lieutenant Commander Richard Byrd (who had flown over the North Pole) and French flying ace René Fonck readied their large, multiple-engine aircraft and crews. Newspapers touted the race, pumping "Atlantic fever" into the minds of Americans and Europeans.

Into this melee stepped a quiet, handsome, confident aviator, who proposed to fly alone in a small, single-engine airplane. Backed by a consortium of St. Louis businessmen, he represented the common American, the underdog, whose guts and moxie could conquer staggering odds. He would forego a parachute and a life raft so he could carry more fuel. He'd take five sandwiches with him, explaining, "If I get to Paris I won't need any more, and if I don't get to Paris, I won't need any more, either." Americans adored him.

> *It was over in a blink of an eye, that moment when aviation stirred the modern imagination. Aviation was transformed from reckless to routine in Lindbergh's lifetime. Today the riskiest part of air travel is the drive to the airport, and the airlines use a barrage of stimuli to protect passengers from ennui.*
>
> *—George Will,* THE PURSUIT OF HAPPINESS, AND OTHER SOBERING THOUGHTS

The Race Is On

Although Lindbergh wasn't well-known, he had the advantage of being a superb pilot, with considerable experience in night and foul-weather flying. He had devel-

Lindbergh was the first person to fly nonstop from New York to Paris, but dozens of people had flown across the Atlantic before him. Eight years earlier, in 1919, John Alcock and Arthur Brown flew nonstop from St. John's, Newfoundland, to Clifden, Ireland, in a two-engine airplane.

Lindbergh's SPIRIT OF ST. LOUIS.

Travelers are always discoverers, especially those who travel by air. There are no signposts in the air to show a man has passed that way before. There are no channels marked. The flier breaks each second into new uncharted seas.
—Anne Morrow Lindbergh,
NORTH TO THE ORIENT

oped his uncanny gift for accurately navigating by compass, chart, and the seat of his pants during more than 7,000 flights in five years. He also had a knack for pushing himself and his aircraft to the limits. In fact, Lindbergh held the records for two, three, and then four emergency bailouts. Nonetheless, aviation experts gave him little chance of success, and Lloyd's of London declined to give odds on his undertaking, stating "the risk is too great."

On the night of May 19, 1927, foul weather kept the competitors grounded in New York. But after a sleepless night, Lindbergh received word of a possible break in the weather and decided to coax his airplane into the air. Named after his benefactors, the *Spirit of St. Louis* was essentially a flying gas tank. Lindbergh had helped design the aircraft, insisting that even the nose of the airplane (behind the engine) be filled with fuel. This meant Lindbergh wouldn't be able to see out the front windshield, so he had two periscopes fitted in the side windows.

By the early evening he was reported over St. John's, Newfoundland, headed out over the black, cold Atlantic. With no radio equipment on board, he would not be seen or heard from again for fifteen more hours. That night, the soul, the hopes, and the prayers of the nation were with Lindbergh the same way a later generation would remember the landing on the Moon. He later recounted that he was so tired along the way that he almost fell asleep and came within feet of crashing into the ocean.

Then, on May 21, Lindbergh spotted a fishing boat off the coast of Ireland and literally yelled out his window to ask where he was and which way he should travel. Miraculously, he was only three miles off course. By the time he landed in Paris, 100,000 people had gathered to greet him. He had won the race, the money, and the world's attention.

The Spirit of St. Louis appeared to be made of metal, but in fact it was covered in fabric, lacquered smooth, and painted silver.

Prevailing eastward winds made it much more difficult to fly from Europe back to North America. In 1927 and 1928, seven experienced pilots died in eight failed attempts. In late 1928, Baron Guenther von Huenefeld, Hermann Koehl, and James Fitzmaurice took off in Ireland and crash-landed in Labrador, Canada. It wasn't until September 1930 that Frenchmen Maurice Bellonte and Dieudonni Costes duplicated Lindbergh's flight in reverse.

FIRST TRANSATLANTIC FLIGHT
On May 16–17, 1919, two U.S. Navy officers—Lieutenant Commander Albert C. Read and Lieutenant Walter Hinton—took off from Long Island, New York, in a Curtiss NC–4, landing in the Azores.

An Ordinary Extraordinary Man

However, Lindbergh did not—as the saying goes—live happily ever after. Initially, he was the perfect hero. Showered with unprecedented tributes, including a massive ticker-tape parade in New York City, he seemed unphased by fame.

Convinced that a new era of aviation had arrived, he flew the *Spirit of St. Louis* across the United States, promoting the idea that anyone could fly. He then turned south and traveled throughout Mexico and South America, planning air routes and encouraging air travel. On one of these trips, Lindbergh met Anne Morrow, the daughter of the ambassador to Mexico. After a story-book marriage, the two flew together all over the world.

But the press had an insatiable hunger for Lindbergh; they stalked him and began to make his life a waking nightmare. Worse, in 1932, the couple's infant son was kidnapped and later killed, which Lindbergh blamed on the invasive media attention by the press. Gradually, an icon who had appeared unassailable and perfect became flawed, and a much more complex and disconcerting individual emerged—a study in contradictions.

For instance, in the mid-1930s, the U.S. Army Air Corp sent Lindbergh to tour Germany and report back on the details of the Luftwaffe's growing strength. Ironically, he was so impressed by the Nazis that he essentially supported them until the United States entered World War II. In fact, Lindbergh expressed approval of German society in general, spoke of racial purity, and made anti-Semitic statements. Yet he was a friend of the wealthy, influential, and Jewish Guggenheim family.

Similarly, before the United States entered the war, Lindbergh was the chief spokesperson for the highly isolationist America First organization. But after the attack on Pearl Harbor, he immediately volunteered to fly and fight for his country. However, President Franklin Roosevelt, who mistrusted Lindbergh, denounced him and refused to let him serve. So Lindbergh became a civilian aviation adviser in the South Pacific, where he talked his way into flying combat missions in P-38 fighters, and showed the younger, less experienced pilots how to increase their flying range by 50 percent.

One of Anne Morrow's teachers once described Lindbergh as "really no more than a mechanic. . . . Had it not been for the lone eagle flight, he would now be in charge of a gasoline station on the outskirts of St. Louis." Nevertheless, for all the controversy and contradiction surrounding him, it was Charles Lindbergh who ultimately convinced the public that air travel was more than frivolous daredevil's play. He saw that air travel was the future of commercial transportation.

In the 1950s Lindbergh won the Pulitzer Prize for his book about his famous flight, also called *The Spirit of St. Louis*. And then, in later years, disturbed by threats to the environment, he became a spokesperson for the World Wildlife Fund. "If I had to choose," Lindbergh said, "I would rather have birds than airplanes."

Rutan's super-efficient **VOYAGER**. *(Photograph by Jim Sugar)*

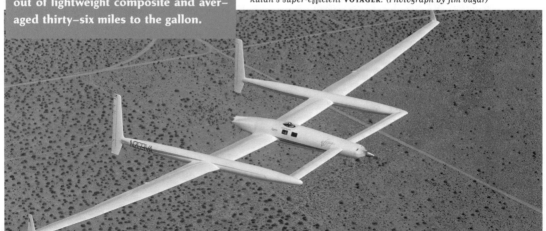

Amelia Earhart circa 1920.

Amelia Earhart (1897–1937), undeniably the most famous female aviator in history, initially achieved celebrity as the first woman to fly across the Atlantic Ocean in 1928, a year after Lindbergh's historic flight. Interestingly, she was only a passenger on the flight, which was flown by two other experienced pilots and set up as a publicity stunt by George Putnam (whom she eventually married). However, four years later she proved herself an able pilot by flying solo, nonstop, across the Atlantic. No other pilot since Lindbergh had accomplished this feat, and President Hoover presented her with an award from the National Geographic Society. Then, in 1935, Earhart became the first person to fly solo, nonstop, from Hawaii to California.

Dubbed "Lady Lindy" (perhaps in part because she bore a somewhat uncanny resemblance to Charles Lindbergh), Earhart was hired by Transcontinental Air Transport (later called TWA) to help convince more women to fly as passengers. In 1937, she set off with experienced navigator Fred Noonan in a Lockheed Electra aircraft to become the first woman to fly around the world, and a member of the first team to fly an equatorial route (the longest path around the globe). After twenty-eight stops and 19,000 miles of the 24,500–mile journey, Earhart and Noonan took off from New Guinea toward Hawaii, with a scheduled stop on Howland Island. They never arrived, and the Electra was never found.

While it's likely that the aircraft flew off course and ran out of fuel over the ocean, it's unlikely that anyone will ever know for sure what befell them. Today, more people know Earhart for her mysterious disappearance than for her spectacular records of the 1930s.

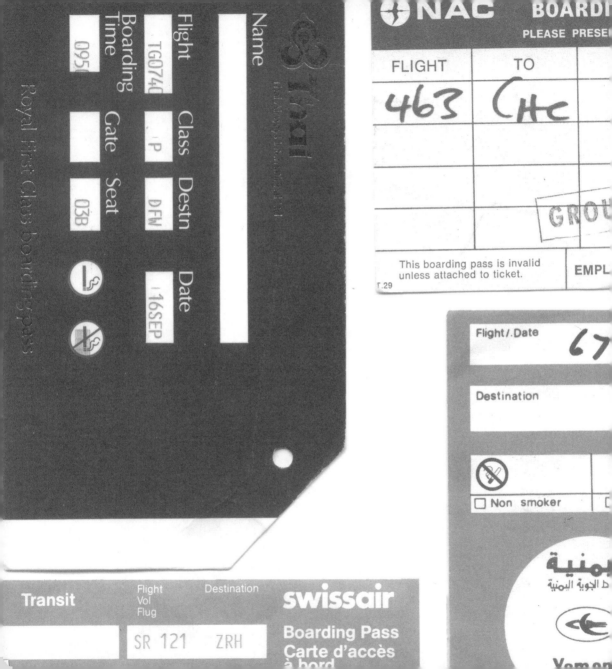

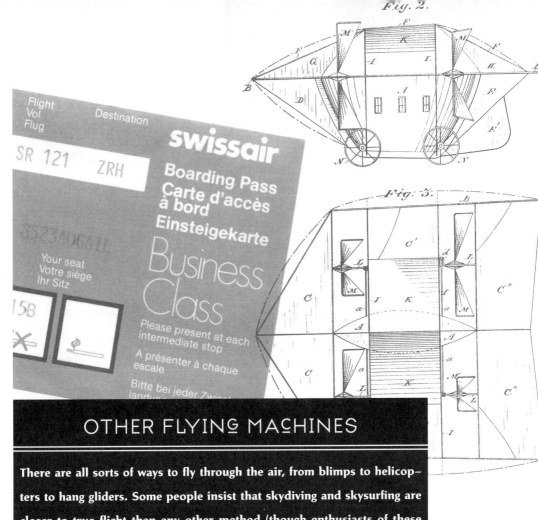

OTHER FLYING MACHINES

There are all sorts of ways to fly through the air, from blimps to helicopters to hang gliders. Some people insist that skydiving and skysurfing are closer to true flight than any other method (though enthusiasts of these two sports tend to fly toward the ground more frequently than other fliers). The next two chapters look at airships and helicopters, as well as a somewhat fanciful idea that hasn't quite "taken off" yet: the aircar.

AIRSHIPS AND HELICOPTERS

If you think about it, the strangest thing about airplanes is that their wings don't move. After all, every early aviation pioneer looked to birds to uncover the secrets of flight. However, one by one they failed at imitating the birds' techniques and finally settled on a design that relies on thrusting a fixed wing through the air fast enough to generate lift.

Nevertheless, even though fixed-wing aircraft come in all sorts of shapes and sizes—from hang gliders to improbable behemoths that carry cargo and look like they'll never get off the ground—they aren't the only way to fly. There are many other methods to travel from place to place through the air, the most important of which are airships and helicopters.

Naval Air Station, Lakehurst, New Jersey, 1924.

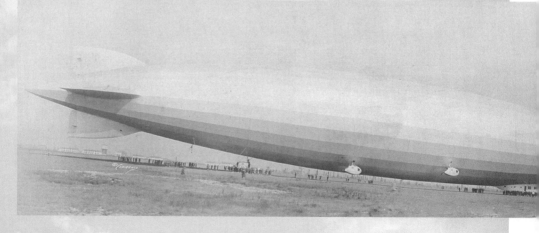

Airships

An airship is basically any balloon that is filled with something lighter than air—usually helium, hydrogen, or hot air—and that uses power to navigate, like the Goodyear or Fuji blimps. Whereas a *dirigible* (from the Latin *dirigere*, "to steer") is an airship that has a rigid or semirigid frame, a *blimp* doesn't.

Built with paper by the Montgolfier brothers in France, the first hot-air balloon floated into the sky in 1783, carrying a sheep, a rooster, and a duck. Of course, hot-air and other nonpowered balloons travel wherever the wind takes them, so they're not technically airships. It wasn't until 1852 that a cigar-shaped balloon was fitted with a steam engine that propelled it along at about five miles per hour. In 1900, the German count Ferdinand von Zeppelin began to build rigid-framed dirigibles for the army, and his design was so successful that even today some people call airships *zeppelins*.

The dirigible, which began to carry passengers in 1910, was an amazingly safe form of air travel for its time, and traveling on one was typically a luxurious affair, with gourmet meals served at fancy tables by waiters. Unfortunately, after

AIRSHIPS AND HELICOPTERS • 217

logging over 1 million miles and safely carrying tens of thousands of passengers, the passenger airships abruptly ceased operating in 1937 when the *Hindenburg* burst into flames over Lakehurst, New Jersey. Even though the majority of passengers survived that disaster, the film and photographs of the hydrogen-filled dirigible exploding were enough to turn any future ticket buyers away from airships and toward the increasingly safe passenger airplane industry.

Nevertheless, airships have certain characteristics that make them ideal for some jobs. For example, on just the amount of fuel it takes a large passenger jet to taxi from the gate to the runway, an airship can fly for fifty hours. Remember that airplanes must burn fuel to stay aloft, whereas airships only need to burn fuel to navigate. So during World War II, the U.S. military used dozens of airships to patrol large expanses of ocean over long periods of time.

Airships, which are today filled with nonflammable helium gas rather than hydrogen, are also extremely well suited for carrying heavy loads of cargo, especially when the items are physically large (like construction materials for a bridge or a modular disaster-relief hospital) and must be moved to or from places that have no railroad tracks or runways. One German company, CargoLifter, is currently building an enormous dirigible—nearly as long as three football fields—that can carry up to 160 tons (352,000 pounds or 160,000 kg).

Helicopters

Igor Sikorsky (1889-1972) was one of those early-twentieth-century aviation pioneers who was inspired by birds, but the bird he wanted to emulate was the hummingbird,

The word helicopter derives from two Greek words: *heliko* (spiral) and *pteron* (wing).

which can fly in any direction at will—even backward—or hover in midair. While Sikorsky initially gained world fame in Russia in 1913 by building the first multiengine airplane, his heart was always drawn to the idea of the helicopter.

Though he didn't actually invent it (there were dozens of other people working in the field), Sikorsky is known today as the father of the modern helicopter because of his innovative advances in technology, especially that of the tail rotor. To understand this achievement, you must first understand the way that helicopters fly.

Both airplanes and helicopters use engines to move a set of wings through the air. The shape of the wing and the angle at which it "attacks" the air cause air to be pushed down, which in turn causes the aircraft to move upward. In a helicopter, the wings are called *blades* or *rotors*, and they spin in a circle, pushing air down around all sides of the aircraft.

The problem with a set of enormous, rotating blades is that as they turn clockwise, something has to stop the helicopter from turning counterclockwise. Whereas some helicopters use a second set of rotors that turn in the opposite direction than the first, Sikorsky's novel approach was to add smaller rotating blades on the helicopter's tail—mounted sideways to the main rotors—which push the tail of the helicopter counterclockwise.

This precise balance of forces, which keeps the helicopter from spinning wildly out of control, is only one of the many incredibly delicate balances that must be maintained during flight. For instance, while an airplane pilot can cruise along with one finger on the controls (or even hands-free for a while, even without autopilot), a helicopter pilot must use both hands and both feet to fly well.

> *The helicopter has become the most universal vehicle ever created and used by man. It approaches closer than any other to fulfillment of mankind's ancient dreams of the flying horse and the magic carpet.*
> —*Igor Sikorsky, father of the modern helicopter*

> *The helicopter has never achieved much success and . . . may be classed with the ornithopter as obsolete.*
> —*Major Oliver Stewart, Royal Air Force, 1928*

> **A normal, medium-sized helicopter with four blades must rotate these "movable wings" at around 258 revolutions per minute (RPM). However, different helicopters use different rotation speeds, depending on factors such as weight, blade width and length, and number of blades.**

Helicopters and airships aren't the only vehicles that can lift straight up off the ground. Some airplanes, too, fall into this category, called VTOLs (Vertical Take Off and Landing aircraft). For instance, the Hawker Harrier is a jet airplane that can direct its high-thrust exhaust downward, which literally pushes the airplane straight up. Then it can direct the air forward in order to fly backward. Similarly, the Bell/Boeing Osprey looks like a helicopter at liftoff and landing, but during flight it can pivot its rotors forward to become a propeller airplane.

One hand is always on the *collective*, which controls both the engine speed and the vertical position of the helicopter by changing the angle of the rotors. The other hand is on the *cyclic*, which controls the helicopter's direction (forward, backward, left, and right) by actually tilting the whole rotor assembly in the direction the pilot wants to travel. Helicopter pilots use their feet to control the tail rotor, which lets them pivot to the left or right.

Airplane purists tend to denigrate helicopters as clunky devices that just barely hold together, and insist that helicopters don't fly, they just "beat the air into submission." In fact, there's a common joke among airplane pilots that helicopters stay in the air because they're so ugly that the Earth repels them. However, the truth is that helicopters are extremely well-designed vehicles that can perform in ways beyond the scope of airplanes, like hovering long enough to rescue people from the ocean, the jungle, or the tops of buildings.

On the other hand, airplanes have a distinct advantage when it comes to speed. Helicopters simply can't fly very fast because of the intense strain on the rotating blades at high speeds: As the helicopter gains speed, the forward-moving rotor approaches the speed of sound, which can cause dangerous vibrations.

The thing is, helicopters are different from planes. An airplane by its nature wants to fly, and if not interfered with too strongly by unusual events or by a deliberately incompetent pilot, it will fly. A helicopter does not want to fly. It is maintained in the air by a variety of forces and controls working in opposition to each other, and if there is any disturbance in this delicate balance the helicopter stops flying; immediately and disastrously. There is no such thing as a gliding helicopter.

This is why being a helicopter pilot is so different from being an airplane pilot, and why in generality, airplane pilots are open, clear-eyed, buoyant extroverts and helicopter pilots are brooding, introspective, anticipators of trouble. They know if something bad has not happened it is about to.

—Newscaster Harry Reasoner

Opposite: Igor Sikorsky flying his VS300. (Courtesy of Igor and Karen Sikorsky)

THE AIRCAR AND
OTHER ODDITIES

At first glance, it seems like a good idea: Take the two most common modes of powered transportation—the car and the airplane—and combine them into a vehicle that you can both drive and fly. After all, cars and aircraft share some key features: a steering control, an engine, fuel, wheels, and a place for passengers and their luggage. The idea isn't a new one: The first hybrid, called the Curtis Autoplane, appeared in 1917, only nine years after Henry Ford's Model T and fourteen years after the Wright brother's first flight.

So why is it that flying cars are in the movies instead of on the road? The problem is that coupling a car and an airplane becomes a study in compromises. For example, wings and a propeller can be detached for driving, but where do you store them? Some inventors suggested putting them in huge airport lockers, while others built trailers so that you could haul the wings from place to place. At least one inventor has even built a set of telescoping wings that could retract when not needed, á la *Chitty Chitty Bang Bang*.

A bigger concern, however, is that most cars are simply too heavy to be airplanes. A road-worthy car must have bumpers and mirrors, not to mention a drivetrain and catalytic converter—all just dead weight once you're flying.

Nevertheless, inventors have long tried for the perfect balance of car and airplane. It seems that every conceivable name has been used: the ConVairCar, the Sky Car, the Aerocar, the Bertelson Aeromobile, and the Waterman Arrowbile. In fact, over seventy-five patents have been granted for "roadable aircraft," ten of them since 1989. Many flew, but none could both fly and drive well.

But that doesn't stop people bitten by the aircar bug, who continue to tinker with lightweight composite materials, publish articles with titles like "The Advanced Personal Fixed-Wing Converticar," and insist that an inexpensive "roadable" aircraft—safe and easy enough for the general public to operate—is just around the corner. As Moulton "Molt" Taylor, inventor of the Aerocar, put it shortly before his death in 1995: "If it weren't for us nuts, you'd still be reading from candlelight and wearing button shoes. . . . The flying automobile is the future. It has to be, just as sure as they made wagons without horses."

> Mark my word: a combination airplane and motorcar is coming. You may smile, but it will come.
>
> —Henry Ford, 1940

> I bought a brand new Aeromobile. Custom made, 'twas a Flight de Ville
>
> —lyrics from the 1956 Chuck Berry song "You Can't Catch Me"

On July 2, 1982, Larry Walters attached forty-two helium-filled balloons to an aluminum chair, sat down holding a pellet pistol and a portable CB radio, and took off from his girlfriend's backyard in the suburbs of Los Angeles. After unexpectedly rising about 16,000 feet, he started shooting out the balloons to land. He did fly for about ninety minutes but ended up knocking out an entire neighborhood's electricity when the balloons became tangled in power lines. He was finally fined $1,500 and charged with the reckless operation of an aircraft "for which there is not currently in effect an airworthiness certificate."

POPULAR MECHANICS *magazine, February 1951.*

EPILOGUE:
THE FUTURE OF
FLYING

One hundred years ago, only a handful of people even believed that powered flight was possible. Today, flying is the safest form of transportation in the world (other than the elevator), there are more than 700,000 licensed private pilots in the United States alone, and each year airlines carry more than 1.6 billion passengers around the world—one-fifth of the world's population. Industry analysts believe that this number will double by 2015 and possibly triple by 2025.

Yet even today air travel is too often arduous. Airport hubs are saturated with aircraft and passengers. There are record-setting delays and cancellations due to everything from weather (even when the weather is nowhere near your flight) to overwhelmed air traffic control systems. Each year flying becomes more like riding a bus, and people now complain about the airlines almost as often as they do lawyers and home-remodeling contractors. If the analysts are right about the future, some radical changes must come about in the airline industry.

Changing the System

Building one or more additional runways at a number of the world's busiest airports would go a long way toward helping air traffic congestion, but as much as people want easier and cheaper travel, few want a new runway in their backyard. The U.S. Federal Aviation Administration has made several big-budget attempts to upgrade its systems, with varying degrees of success. Some companies, like Southwest Airlines, now fly mostly short point-to-point trips, largely bypassing the often-frustrating hub-and-spoke system (which routes people through major airports such as those in Chicago, Frankfurt, or Hong Kong in order to get to other destination cities).

> When once you have tasted flight, you will forever walk the Earth with your eyes turned skyward, for there you have been and there you will always long to return.
>
> —Leonardo da Vinci

James Fallows, in his book *Free Flight,* suggests an even more dramatic change is to come. Fallows points out that almost every major industry, from personal computers to retail shopping, has moved toward making their wares more personalized and convenient to the customer. The airline industry, however, still largely revolves around conveniencing the airlines themselves. He contends that in the near future large fleets of high-tech air taxis, holding four or five passengers each, will be able to fly you directly between airports you choose avoiding hubs. Even better, these small aircraft, which are nowhere near as loud as large jets, will be able to use any of the more than 3,500 small airports that already exist in communities around the United States. If these aircraft can be shown to be as safe and affordable as the big airliners, many people will jump at the chance for this sort of convenience.

In fact, many businesspeople are already defecting to this model, chartering private jets instead of wasting their executives' time muddling through one hub after another. Today, you can charter a business jet for about the same cost as buying four or five first-class tickets on an airliner. Future air taxis would likely bring costs down much further.

New Technology

Of course, there will always be a need for larger jets, too, so Boeing and Airbus are hard at work shaping the future of commercial flight. At the time of this writing,

Airbus is building what will become the world's biggest airliner, the double-decker, 555-seat, four-engine Airbus 380. This aircraft will likely go into service in 2006 and provide the first real competition to the Boeing 747 for large-scale hauling of passengers and cargo.

While NASA is best known for its work in space, it is also very active in aviation research, including developing new lightweight composite materials, revamping air traffic control systems, and building "smart" airplanes that can fly themselves in emergency situations. Some researchers are even exploring how an airplane's outer skin could actually change shape at different phases of a flight, mimicking birds by narrowing and sweeping back the wings at higher speeds.

NASA's technology probably won't show up in the public sector until 2030 or so. That's likely the same time that someone will figure out how to make a cost-effective supersonic airliner, making continent-hopping easier than ever. For shorter trips, however, some innovators point to the future of personal aviation: aircraft as big as today's sport utility vehicles that use small jet engines to take off vertically from your driveway, and use a grid of wirelessly networked computers to avoid smashing into one another.

Back from the Future

Of course, it's easier to dream wildly about the future than to sit back and really experience the present. If poetry is the act of distilling some mysterious deep truth from the dross of the everyday world, then the act of a great aluminum beast taking off and flying over our familiar landscape is, indeed, poetry.

While most passengers are content to eat dinner and watch a movie, ignoring the fact that they're hurtling across the sky, others find it miraculous. Flying is one of the most astonishing things humans have ever learned to do. It is the culmination of thousands of years of dreaming while watching the birds with envy and wonder.

So it's true that airports are a hassle, and that airplane food isn't great. It's true that luggage misses connections, that turbulence can be scary, that the air is dehydrating, and that very, very rarely something goes terribly wrong. But the next time you find yourself worrying or fuming, remember how amazing it is that we have tamed the powerful air, riding it like the waves of a great invisible ocean. It is poetry in motion.

APPENDIX
IDENTIFYING
AIRPLANES:
A FIELD GUIDE

TWO JET ENGINES

Both Engines on the Rear of the Fuselage

Full-size Jet

McDonnell Douglas DC-9, MD-80

Boeing 717 (which was originally called the MD-95)

Telltale signs: There aren't many DC-9s or 717s in service, so it's probably an MD-80. The horizontal stabilizer on the tail of these three aircraft is at the top of the tail, forming a *T*. Also, the end of the fuselage on the MD-80 and Boeing 717 looks like a flathead screwdriver. The Boeing 717 is much shorter and stubbier than the MD-80 and holds only about 100 passengers.

Small Commuter Jet (fewer than 100 passenters)

EMB-145: This popular jet has a distinctive pointed nose, reminiscent of the Concorde.

Fokker F28, F70, and F100: These jets have a rounded nose, and the tail extends farther forward than in most aircraft.

Canadair Challenger: This jet has a shorter fuselage than the others, and it may have winglets.

British Aerospace One-Eleven: The engines on this jet are mounted slightly lower than the windows.

Small Corporate Jet

Among the most common business jets are the Gulfstream, the Learjet, and the Cessna Citation. Business jets are often difficult to distinguish from each other from a distance.

Both Engines Mounted on the Wings

Wide-body Airplane

Airbus A300, A310, A330

Boeing 767, 777

Telltale signs: The wide-body, "twin aisle" aircraft are significantly larger than the narrow-body "single aisle" airplanes. The Airbus aircraft all have small winglets at the end of their wings (the Boeing aircraft do not), and the fuselage extends out farther (and straighter) behind the tailfin than in the 767. The Airbus A330 and the Boeing 777 are almost identical in length and wingspan, but the Airbus has winglets, and the end of the fuselage on the 777 looks like a flathead screwdriver. Also, the 777 has three pairs of tires on each landing gear, whereas the 767 has only two.

The A300 and A310 are very similar, though the A310 is shorter, making it appear more squat, like the Boeing 767.

Narrow-body Airplane

Airbus A319, A320

Boeing 737, 757

Telltale signs: Twin-engine narrow-bodies are significantly slimmer and smaller than wide-body aircraft. The Airbus A320 has tiny up-and-down winglets at the end of its wings, and the end of the fuselage extends out longer behind the tailfin than in the Boeing airplanes. The biggest differences between the 737 and the 757 are the size (the 757 is about one-third longer than the 737) and the end of the fuselage (where the 757 comes almost to a point, the 737 is cut off at an angle, like a calligraphy pen). The engines on all but the earliest 737s are also slightly "squashed" at the bottom.

THREE JET ENGINES

All Three Engines on or Around the Tail of the Plane

Boeing 727

Tupolev Tu-154

Yakovlev Yak-40

Telltale signs: It's most likely a Boeing 727. The Russian-made Tupolev Tu-154 has a prominent antenna protruding forward from the tail. The Yakovlev Yak-40 is a very small, stubby airplane.

One Engine on Each Wing, and One in Tail

Lockheed TriStar L-1011 ("el ten-eleven")
McDonnell Douglas DC-10, MD-11

Telltale signs: The most obvious difference between the Lockheed and Mc-Donnell Douglas models is that the front of the tail engine on the L-1011 is higher than its back. (The air intake is above the fuselage, and the exhaust comes out the back of the fuselage itself.) On the DC-10 and MD-11, the exhaust is directly behind the air intake, as on most other engines. Note that the MD-11 has winglets at the end of its wings and is longer than the DC-10.

FOUR JET ENGINES

Wings Extend from the Bottom of the Airplane

If the wings extend from the lower part of the fuselage, it's probably an Airbus A340, Boeing 707, Boeing 747, Ilyushin IL-86, Ilyushin IL-96, or a McDonnell Douglas DC-8.

Wide-body Aircraft

Airbus A340

Boeing 747

Telltale signs: The Boeing 747 is an enormous wide-body plane and has a distinctive hump in the front part of the fuselage. The Airbus A340 has winglets that stick up at the end of the wings (though more recent 747s also have winglets). Plus, the end of the fuselage on this large wide-body airplane extends out to a bluntly pointed tip.

Narrow-body Aircraft

Boeing 707

McDonnell Douglas DC-8

Telltale signs: These long and narrow aircrafts are similar though the 707 has a distinctive antenna pointing forward at the top of the tail fin. Also, the DC-8 has much narrower wings.

Wings Extend from the Top of the Airplane

This type of jet is pretty rare; it's likely an Antonov An-124, Avro RJ/British Aerosapce 146, or a Lockheed C-5 Galaxy. The Avro RJ/British Aerospace 146 is a pretty small, somewhat stubby airplane. The Lockheed C-5 Galaxy and the Antonov An-124 are enormous and are used almost exclusively for cargo and military operations.

Currently the largest aircraft in the world, the Antonov An–225, has three engines on each wing and two vertical stabilizers (forming an H). It also has seven pairs of wheels on each side, plus four nose wheels, in order to carry a total weight of over 1.3 million pounds (600,000 kg).

FOR MORE INFORMATION

If this book has inspired you to learn more about flying, you're in luck—there are literally thousands of books, magazines, and Web sites devoted to aviation. To make the search easier, your first step should be the Flying Book Web Site, at *http://www.theflyingbook.com*, which has links and an extended bibliography of resources.

However, if you're browsing through the shelves at your local bookstore or library, here's a list of some of the best books on the subject.

Anderson, David and Scott Eberhardt. *Understanding Flight*. New York: McGraw Hill, 2001. Although it's a physics textbook, this book is a great resource for anyone who wants to understand aerodynamics.

Berk, William and Frank Berk. *Guide to Airport Airplanes*. Plymouth, Mich.: Plymouth Press, 1996. A great book to have on hand at an airport if you like identifying commercial airplanes.

Cronin, John. *Your Flight Questions Answered by a Jetliner Pilot*. Vergennes, Vt.: Plymouth Press, 1998. Basic and to the point, but provides a lot of detailed information and terminology.

Dalton, Stephen. *The Miracle of Flight*. Buffalo, N.Y.: Firefly Books, 1999. Stunning photographs and illustrations of birds, insects, and other flying objects make this book a must have.

English, Dave. *Slipping the Surly Bonds*. New York: McGraw-Hill, 1998. A collection of terrific quotations about airplanes, based on a popular aviation Web site.

Evans, Julien. *All You Ever Wanted to Know About Flying*. Osceola, Wis.: Motorbooks, Intl., 1997. A highly llustrated little book with technical explanations on airliners and airports.

Ridley, Layne. *White Knuckles*. New York: Doubleday & Co., 1987. This is my favorite book for fearful flyers; it's not only informative, but fun to read, too.

Seaman, Debbie. *The Fearless Flier's Handbook*. Berkeley, Calif.: Ten Speed Press, 1998. Based on Quantas Airlines' fear of flying clinic, but interesting to almost any passenger.

Sternstein, Ed and Todd Gold. *From Takeoff to Landing*. New York: Pocket Books, 1991. Lots of details about flying you never knew you wanted to know.

Wright, Orville. *How We Invented the Airplane*. Mineola, N.Y.: Dover Publications, 1991. Although often too technical and dry, this little book has great photographs and it's fun to hear the history in Orville Wright's own words.

ART CREDITS

INDEX